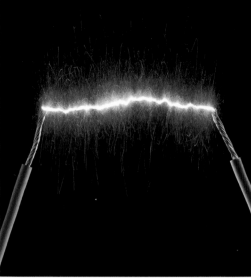

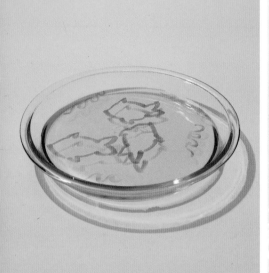

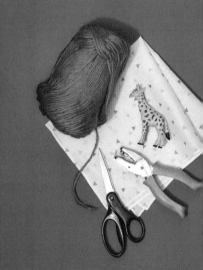

GOOD HOUSEKEEPING

AMAZING SCIENCE

83 Hands-On S.T.E.A.M. Experiments for Curious Kids!

by **Aubre Andrus**

with **Rachel Rothman**

Chief Technologist and Engineering Director
Good Housekeeping Institute

KIDS

HEARST

HOME

CONTENTS

JOIN THE S.T.E.A.M. TEAM

Amazing Science invites you into the ultimate laboratory: the world around you. In more than 80 experiments, you'll explore everyday science—both indoors and out—that we hope you'll find inspiring, surprising, and loads of fun.

The experiments in this book cover important topics: Science, Technology, Engineering, Art, and Math (also called S.T.E.A.M.). The world of science is vast, and most investigations cover more than one of these. Read these tips and get ready to have an awesome experience.

To find an experiment on a particular topic, check out the S.T.E.A.M. Index on page 154.

Think Like a Scientist

All journeys of exploration begin with a question such as why or how or what if? Finding the answer through a series of steps is called the **scientific method**. First, you'll **observe**, or take a look at something that's going on in your world and come up with an idea about what is happening. Then you'll **ask a question** about your observation, what it is that you want to know. You'll **make a hypothesis**, which is an educated guess, about the answer to your question and how it can be tested. Then you'll **design an experiment** to test your hypothesis. During the experiment, you'll observe what happens and record the results. Then you'll **evaluate the results** and draw a conclusion: Was your hypothesis right or wrong? If an experiment doesn't turn out the way a scientist predicted, the process can begin all over again. What is your new theory based on prior results? How will you **test it again**?

HI, I'M RACHEL! EVERY DAY I GET TO PUT ON MY SCIENTIST HAT AND TACKLE NEW PROJECTS. I TEST THE LATEST AND GREATEST SMART HOME PRODUCTS, VEHICLES, AND TOYS. I ALSO GATHER AND INTERPRET DATA SO THAT WE CAN GIVE OUR READERS WHAT THEY WANT!

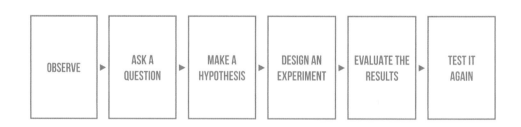

OBSERVE ▶ ASK A QUESTION ▶ MAKE A HYPOTHESIS ▶ DESIGN AN EXPERIMENT ▶ EVALUATE THE RESULTS ▶ TEST IT AGAIN

Take Notes

In each experiment, you'll use a **notebook** to keep track of your predictions, observations, and results and be able to refer back to them later on if you want to try the experiment again. (Any lined notebook will do!)

Read the Experiments

Before you begin any experiment, read it over first. Each starts with a note about what it investigates, includes a list of materials you'll need, guides you through the instructions, and offers an explanation. Nearly all the materials are common items that are easy to find. You'll find bonus experiments and special tips, too.

 There are different **levels of difficulty**. Some experiments will be easy for you, others may be more challenging and require additional support, and a few may need adult help.

 Some experiments have the potential to be **messier** than others. For high-mess experiments, you'll need to protect your work space, work outside, or have clean-up supplies handy.

 Some experiments will take 15 or 30 minutes start to finish, and others may need more **time** to show results.

MYSTERY SOLVED! Once you've completed an experiment, you can compare your analysis with this explanation of the scientific principles at work and why the experiment turned out the way it did.

TAKE 2! These experiments are variations on the main experiments and encourage you to set up your own tests following the scientific method.

Turn the page to begin your science adventure. The most important tip of all—get ready to have fun!

—Rachel Rothman
Chief Technologist and Engineering Director
Good Housekeeping Institute

MEET THE EXPERTS

The engineers, scientists, and product analysts at the Good Housekeeping Institute test thousands of products every year in six state-of-the-art labs. Learn about the scientists and experts who have been involved in bringing this book to you and making sure it has earned the century-old Good Housekeeping Seal. To learn more, go to *goodhousekeeping.com/institute*.

Birnur Aral, PhD
Director, Health, Beauty & Environmental Sciences Lab

My advice for young scientists: I believe we all start out as little scientists when we are trying to understand the world around us. If you can hang on to that natural curiosity, you will make an excellent scientist.

Why innovation matters to me: Innovation excites me. It's typically the result of great teamwork with team members applying knowledge from different fields of study to solve a real problem.

Carolyn Forte
Director, Home Appliances & Cleaning Products Lab

The most extreme testing technique I've used: Our automated vacuum cleaner tester lets us measure how much embedded dirt a vacuum cleaner removes from carpeting, almost without lifting a finger. Without it, we'd have to do the vacuuming by hand.

The best at-home tip I learned from testing: Stay on top of stains and grime. The longer it sits, the harder it is to remove.

"Our job is to deliver trusted advice on the best of the best." —Laurie Jennings

Laurie Jennings
GH Institute Director

What it's like to lead a team of scientists that includes engineers, chemists, and home care specialists: I love working with this group of super-smart scientists. They are constantly teaching me new facts and challenging me to look at things in new ways—and they certainly keep me on my toes! One of the most fun parts of my job is translating their genius into stories that appear in our magazine and online. It's so satisfying to hear from readers how much our advice helps them in their lives.

Why we test products for consumers: Just as the GH Institute began over 100 years ago as an experiment station to protect consumers from bad or dangerous products, we carry on that mission today. Our job is to deliver trusted advice on the best of the best. Plus, it's one of the most fun things you could do for a living!

Kate Merker
Chief Food Director

How I started cooking: I have always loved to cook. My father and I used to embark on these incredibly long and labor-intensive cooking projects together—my all-time favorite was rugelach. And as a little girl I spent hours in my grandparents' restaurant in Queens, New York. My grandfather gave me my first job. He paid me 25 cents extra if more salt went into the shaker than onto the table.

My favorite food to test: Developing a recipe for vegan chocolate chip cookies was a huge hit with our team. There were five variations we tested and retested. We explored which type of sugar to use (brown, granulated, or a combination), we tasted three types of chocolate chips (milk, semisweet, and bittersweet), and then we looked at cookie size, oven temperature, and bake time to get the ultimate chewy chocolate chip cookie. It is so good that it rivals recipes with butter and eggs.

Nicole Papantoniou
Deputy Director, Kitchen Appliances & Technology Lab

The most unusual appliance I ever tested: At the time, the thought of a pressure cooker that could also air fry was questionable, but it tested very well and was impressive.

My favorite new technology: I love having access to quality recipe apps on my phone. Bookmarking favorites into a virtual recipe box is a treat.

Rachel Rothman
Chief Technologist and Engineering Director, and self-described Gadget Girl

Why I do experiments with my toddlers: I love fostering a sense of wonderment and curiosity in my kids. The excitement they feel when they see everyday "magic" never dulls for me. I find experimentation to be a beautiful way to teach my kids problem-solving skills and empower them.

Why I love science: Science is everywhere! Having a better understanding of scientific principles allows me to better solve everyday problems in clever ways. From cooking and playing to the clothes we wear and the furniture we sit on, science is at play!

Lexie Sachs
Textiles Director

How I learned about fabric-based products: I studied fiber science in college, which combined chemistry and engineering with classes on fashion and fabric. I learned everything from how fabrics are made to how they react in different environments. After college, I worked in product development in the fashion and home industries, to help bring the ideas from designers into the hands of shoppers.

The best thing I learned from test results: You do not have to spend a lot of money to get a good product. Sometimes the less expensive fabric-based products perform better in our tests than the pricier ones, so we can help readers understand how to get the best value when they shop.

Stefani Sassos, MS, RDN
Registered Dietitian

How I use science in my work and life: Nutrients give our body instructions on how to function, so I use science every day to figure out ways that we can support a healthy body through the foods we choose to eat.

My science superpower would be: X-ray vision to see the superpowers inside fruits and veggies.

Sabina Wizemann
Senior Chemist

How I work with the different labs: I make solutions other labs can use for their testing. For example, textile engineers test how fabrics behave when they touch sweat, and determine if your favorite jersey will fade or stain. I can make a sweat solution in my lab; I know it sounds yucky, but I think collecting real sweat from people is doubly yucky.

My advice about conducting experiments: When it comes to experiments, planning is everything. I like to think of it as being able to predict the future. I try to imagine all the different scenarios (good and bad) and also ask as many questions as I can think of before I start. The more prepared I am, the more time I have to observe any changes and make conclusions, which is the most fun.

"Science is everywhere! Having a better understanding of scientific principles allows me to better solve everyday problems in clever ways." —Rachel Rothman

CORE CONCEPTS
States of Matter

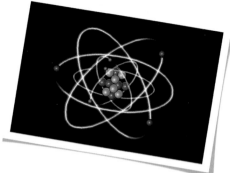

Everything we see is made of atoms—including you! **Atoms** are tiny particles that are way too small to see. When two or more atoms combine, they create **molecules**. When molecules bond together, they create **matter**. Matter is anything that takes up space. There are three main states of matter: solid, liquid, and gas. **Density** is a way to measure how tightly the molecules are packed together.

SOLID Anything that's rigid, feels hard, and has a clearly defined shape—like a pencil, a bed, or a car—is a solid. The molecules that make up the object are fixed in place, which means the object can't change shape unless large forces are acting on it. Solids are made up of molecules that are packed very tightly together. They are typically the densest type of matter. Wood, sand, and apples are examples of solids.

Solid

LIQUID Milk, oil, water, and similar substances don't have a clearly defined shape. A liquid's molecules move around one another and are bound loosely to each other. A liquid can take on the shape to whatever container it's poured into. However, a liquid does have a fixed volume (the amount of space it takes up).

GAS A gas has no shape and is the least dense type of matter. It can expand or contract depending on conditions it is exposed to, such as heat, which means it does not have a fixed volume. The volume, or amount of space it takes up, can change. Examples of gases include steam (water vapor), the air that we breathe, and the helium that's used to inflate party balloons. Supercharged gas, called plasma, occurs in nature (including stars and lightning) and is used in technology (such as fluorescent lights and some television displays).

Liquid

NOTE IT! Water is the most common substance that exists on Earth in all three states of matter: solid (ice), liquid (water), and gas (water vapor).

Gas

Fogged In

It's no mist-ery why San Francisco's Golden Gate Bridge gets fogged in—it's science! When the moist ocean air meets warmer coastal air, some of the water vapor in the air condenses into fog. To learn more about condensation, check out **Fight the Fog (page 46)**.

Changing States

A substance can change from one state to another under the right circumstances. It's a matter of heat: how the molecules warm up or cool down. You see this happen when your ice cream melts on a warm day, changing a scoop of fudge ripple from a solid into a liquid. Or when a pond freezes up, changing water from a liquid to a solid. But how does the transformation happen?

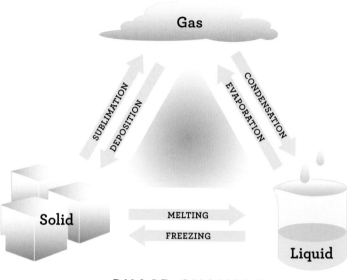

PHASE CHANGES

HEAT When molecules are heated up, they vibrate more quickly and strongly and their temperature increases. As they move around, the space between them increases and the matter (or substance) becomes less dense. Eventually, it changes from one state to another. When a cold icicle is heated up by warmer air, the molecules move apart. The ice starts to melt, changing from a solid to a liquid. The temperature at which a solid becomes a liquid is called the **melting point**. Almost every solid substance has its own melting point, and the melting point for water is 32°F (0°C).

The **boiling point** is the temperature at which a liquid changes to a gas. This transformation happens because as molecules heat up, they move even farther apart. For water, the boiling point—when steam begins to rise—is 212°F (100°C). Other liquids have different boiling points.

COLD When molecules are cooled down, their movement slows and they are drawn closer together. This makes the matter more dense. When gas molecules cool down, they slow down, clump together, and turn into a liquid. This process is called **condensation**, and it's what happens when the bathroom mirror fogs up during your shower. (Explore this phenomenon in **Fight the Fog on page 46**.) Liquids that are cooled down even further become solids. This happens, for example, when the burning-hot lava of a volcano cools and becomes hard rock.

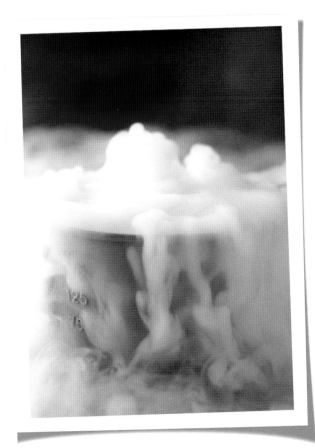

FAST ARRIVAL Some solids can become a gas without becoming a liquid first. This is called **sublimation**. Dry ice is a solid form of carbon dioxide (which is normally a gas). It's super cold (-109.3°F, or -78.5°C), so cold that you can't touch it without getting frostbite. But dry ice doesn't melt into a liquid. As it warms, the ice just looks like it's getting smaller as it turns into a gas. Dry ice can keep food and medicine cold in shipping packages without leaking water as it warms. It's also how fog machines create eerie visual smoky-looking effects without making a watery mess.

Forces and Motion

A force is a push or a pull that makes something move, stop, or change speed or direction. Motion is what happens when an object changes its position or location. But an object won't move unless there is a force applied to it that makes it move.

FRICTION When one surface rubs across another, it creates friction. Friction is a force that pushes in the opposite direction of that in which an object is moving, slowing the object down. Some surfaces have more friction than others. The amount of friction between the bottom of your shoes and a sidewalk helps you walk without slipping. There's less friction between your shoes and the ground when you walk across a sheet of ice. That's why you're more likely to slip. Ball bearings (tiny metal balls) inside a spinning toy reduce friction, just as the wheels on a roller coaster do (see page 112 for more about coasters).

PULLING AND PUSHING If you've ever played with two magnets at once, you know that they will either snap together or push away from each other. That's because opposites attract, and magnets are dipolar—they have positive and negative poles. Magnetism is the invisible force that can attract or repel objects to or from one another. Find out more about how magnets work in **Attract and Repel (page 102)**.

Going Down

Gravity is a force of attraction—it pulls objects toward one another. When you let go of a ball and it falls to the ground—or back into a juggler's hand— that's because of gravity. Gravity is also the force that holds planets like Earth in orbit around the sun. Explore gravity in **Free Falling (page 84)**.

Energy

Energy is the ability to make things move and change. Scientists define it as the ability to do work. There are different types of energy at work in your everyday world. The Law of the Conservation of Energy (LOCOE) states that energy cannot be created or destroyed, it can only be changed from one form of energy to another.

KINETIC AND POTENTIAL ENERGY When an object moves, it has kinetic energy. The faster it moves, the more kinetic energy it has. When an object is staying still, it has potential energy (stored energy). That potential energy decreases or increases based on the position of the object. For example, an object on top of a bookcase will have more potential energy because it has a longer way to fall. As it starts falling—bam!—the energy converts to kinetic energy.

Heat is a form of kinetic energy. When the atoms that make up an object move quickly, they get hotter and have more kinetic energy. The energy from heat can be transferred from a stove through a pot to boil water. Find out what heat can do to a marshmallow in **All Puffed Up (page 30)**.

CHEMICAL ENERGY Energy stored in chemical compounds is called chemical potential energy. Food contains chemical potential energy. When you eat a salad, for example, or any other food, the energy stored in it is released through digestion. Explore chemical reactions in **Presto Change-O (page 28)**.

ELECTRICAL ENERGY Atoms are made up of three major groups of particles: protons, neutrons, and electrons. These particles carry a positive, neutral, or negative charge. When electrons move through matter, they create electricity, which powers toasters and other electrical machines and devices. Learn more about how electrical energy can be used to power a flashlight in **Battery Blast (page 62)**.

MECHANICAL ENERGY Mechanical energy is the energy of motion and energy stored because of its position. It exists in nonmoving objects as potential energy. When you push a book across your desk, you're using mechanical energy and converting the potential energy in the book to kinetic energy. Look into mechanical energy in **Wheel Fun (page 80)**.

WAVE ENERGY Some forms of energy, including light and sound, move as waves. These waves can be short or long (called the wavelength) and fast or slow (called the frequency). Sound waves can't be seen, but they can be heard. Most light waves can't be seen either, except for visible light. That light enables you to see colors all around you. You can create your own light waves in **Light Energy (page 66)** and make your own sound waves in **Good Vibrations (page 88)**.

shorter wavelength
higher frequency
higher energy

longer wavelength
lower frequency
lower energy

Simple Machines

Machines are mechanical devices used to apply a force and do work so you don't have to expend as much effort. What scientists call simple machines don't have a lot of moving parts and they don't need electricity. But they do make work easier, which means you can use less energy to complete a task.

WHEEL AND AXLE The wheel and axle is one of the most important inventions of all time. This simple machine made it possible for humans to build vehicles—carts and chariots—that moved food, people, and supplies more readily than ever before. Wheels reduce friction, because, at any moment, only the very bottom of a wheel touches the ground. Less surface-on-surface contact means less friction. An axle is the rod that goes through the center of a wheel. It allows wheels to turn. Learn more about the wheel and axle in **Wheel Fun (page 80).**

LEVER Levers have a rigid part, called the arm. It is supported by a fulcrum, the point where the lever pivots. Levers make it easier to lift things (like friends on a seesaw). When a force is applied to (pushes down on) one end of a lever, the other end goes up. There are many different kinds of levers, and the fulcrum can be located at the center or closer to one end.

PULLEY A pulley uses the wheel and axle to make lifting easier. In this simple machine, the wheel has a groove in it, and a rope or chain is placed in the groove. When you lift a box using a pulley, you are redirecting the force needed to do the work. Instead of trying to pull the box up, you are just pulling a rope down, and the pulley is doing the bulk of the work.

INCLINED PLANE
A ramp is an example of an inclined plane, a surface with one end higher than the other. This simple machine doesn't move at all, but it still helps when moving an object from a lower to a higher level. Sliding something takes less effort than lifting it, whether you're pushing a box of books up a ramp or shoveling dirt.

SCREW A screw is an inclined plane with a twist—literally. Combined with a rotational force, a screw can move something from a lower position to a higher one. For example, when the bit of a drill rotates in a plank of wood, it moves the wood up the ribs on its shaft (a ramp) and out of the plank. A water screw (also called an Archimedes screw, after its inventor) can move water from a lower level to a higher one, circulating water from the bottom to the top of an amusement park flume ride or a water sports course. Check out everyday screws in **Big Muddy (page 138)** and **Wave Works (page 148)**.

WEDGE A wedge is composed of two inclined planes. It has a pointy tip, a long flat side, and a long inclined side and works when force is applied. You can use a wedge to separate one object into multiple pieces, or to attach one object to another. A wedge can also be used to lift an object or hold it in place. When you press down on an apple slicer, the blades (wedges) cut the fruit in pieces. A pushpin attaches a piece of paper to a corkboard. A doorstop holds a door open (or closed) on a windy day. And a small wedge called a shim, when placed under a too-short table leg, stops it from wobbling. A wedge (knife) is used in **Go, Go, Re-Grow (page 140)** and **Go with the Flow (page 142)**.

PUTTING IT TOGETHER Compound machines are machines that are made from two or more simple machines.

On a pair of scissors, the handles are levers, the blades are wedges, and there is a fulcrum in between. The potential energy in scissors converts to kinetic energy when you apply force—squeeze down on—the handles.

Different types of cranes use simple machines in varying ways. They lift heavy objects using a pulley, move on wheels and axles, and are assembled with screws. A pulley may use a wedge socket to help control the speed of the wire rope running through it, and a tall tower crane has a lever (a beam that balances on a fulcrum). Explore compound machines at work in **Energy from Nature (pages 74 to 75)**.

Fluid Food

Cow's milk has lots of components! It's mostly a combination of fat and water, but it also has proteins (including casein and whey), sugar (lactose), vitamins, and minerals. Water and fat usually separate, but in milk they form an emulsion (a mixture of two or more liquids).

Chapter 1

FOOD SCIENCE

Every time you cook something, you are using science! Our food is made up of building blocks (called molecules) such as water, fats, sugars, and proteins. Different foods can look and taste very different depending on how those molecules interact with one another and whether we heat them up or cool them down. It's a little bit chemistry, a little bit biology, and, hopefully, a lot yummy. Let's head to your laboratory, *er*, kitchen, and start experimenting!

EXPERIMENTS

Rainbow Milk

While many substances, such as sugar and salt, dissolve in water, fats don't. Why not? There's a saying in science that like dissolves like, and water and fats are not alike. Water will not dissolve in fat, and fat won't dissolve in water. What do you think will happen if you introduce soap to a mixture of water and fat? Write down your prediction in your science notebook.

DIFFICULTY: 💪💪💪 **MESS-O-METER:** ✴ ✴ ✴ **TIME: 15 MINUTES**

YOU WILL NEED

Whole milk (about 2 cups/480 ml, depending on the size of your dish)

Shallow baking dish or pie plate

Liquid food coloring (2 or more colors)

Science notebook and pencil

Dish soap (just a drop)

1. Add enough whole milk to cover the bottom of the dish. If it's sloshing a bit, let it settle.

2. Add 3 to 4 drops of each food coloring to the milk. Make sure to add the drops to the center of the dish. (See image A.) What happens when the food coloring touches the milk? Write down your observations in your science notebook.

3. Now add a drop of dish soap into the center of the dish. (See image B.) What happens? Is this what you expected?

4. Watch the milk for another 1 or 2 minutes. (See image C.) Does anything change? Record your observations.

MYSTERY SOLVED!
When you put drops of food coloring in water, it dissolves. That's because they're both liquids, and liquids mix with other liquids. But when you added the food coloring to the milk, which is a combination of liquid and fat, you do not see a reaction. Why did adding soap make such a big change? Soap molecules break up fat—that's why dishwashing liquid cleans a greasy pan. As the soap molecules chase around after the fat molecules in the milk, the food coloring mixes with the water in the milk and is pushed around in an amazing way. This would happen without the food coloring, but you wouldn't see it.

TAKE 2!
Try this experiment using 2% milk. Two percent milk has less fat than whole milk. How do you think the fat content will affect the outcome? Did the colors react more or less than they did in the whole milk? Then try it with heavy cream and observe the differences.

KIDS DRINK ABOUT TWICE AS MUCH MILK AS ADULTS!

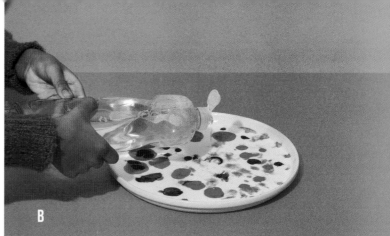

B

Shake-and-Make Butter

How do you turn a liquid into a solid? With water, you freeze it to make ice. But turning milk into butter is more complicated. Milk and butter contain water and fat, and to make butter the fat needs to be separated from the water. Since fat is lighter than water, it rises to the surface and can be skimmed off to make cream. Then you can shake the cream and make your own butter at home. Let's give it a try!

DIFFICULTY: 🤍🤍🤍 **MESS-O-METER:** ✺ ✺ ✺ **TIME: 20 MINUTES**

YOU WILL NEED

- 1 cup (240 ml) heavy whipping cream, at room temperature
- **1 clean pint-size (480 ml) glass jar with a tight-fitting lid**
- **Timer or stopwatch**
- **Science notebook and pencil**
- **Bowl**

→ Take it out of the refrigerator a few hours before you plan to start.

1. Pour the room-temperature cream into the jar. Screw the lid on tightly.

2. Start your timer. Now start shaking the jar. You'll hear the liquid sloshing around. If your arm gets tired, you can switch hands, but keep on shaking it.

3. When the sloshing stops, that means the liquid is thicker, like whipped cream. How did this happen? Tiny air bubbles in the jar became trapped in the cream, thickening it. Adding a pinch of sugar and vanilla extract to this whipped cream would make it taste great on top of a dessert. But to make butter, you need to keep shaking.

4. Continue to shake the jar until you hear sloshing again. That means the air bubbles in the whipped cream have now collapsed and the fat molecules (butterfat) are separating from the liquid (buttermilk) and beginning to clump together.

5. Keep shaking until you hear a ball of butter thudding against the sides. Look inside the jar—the butter will be pale yellow, and there will be just a little bit of leftover liquid that is milky white. Stop your timer and note the time in your science notebook. Do you think it would take more or less time if you shook the jar faster or slower?

6. Pour out the remaining liquid into a bowl and examine your results. How much liquid is there? When you shook up the heavy cream, the fat molecules separated from the liquid. They clumped together and eventually formed solid butter.

7. Store the butter in a clean covered container in the refrigerator. It will last for 1 week, and you can spread it on your toast, just like the store-bought kind!

8. The leftover liquid is called buttermilk. Buttermilk is used to make ranch dressing and is sometimes added to pancakes, mashed potatoes, or muffins. Taste it. What is the flavor like? What is the consistency (thick or thin)? Write down your observations in your science notebook.

MYSTERY SOLVED!
Butter is at least 80% fat. Whole milk is mostly water, with about 3% to 4%t fat. Heavy cream is 36% fat, a much better ratio (amount of fat to liquid) for making butter.

TAKE 2!
When molecules in cream are shaken, they heat up. That means they have more energy and they move faster. Knowing this, do you think cold cream will turn into butter faster than room temperature cream? What you think is going to happen, based on the facts you have so far, is called your theory. Test your theory: Use cold cream to make butter and time it. Write up this second experiment—and its results—in your science notebook and then compare it to the first experiment.

NOTE IT!
Milk we drink has been homogenized—a process that prevents the fat from separating from the liquid.

Presto Change-O

Kitchen chemistry is at work when two different kinds of ingredients meet—an acid and a base. Acids taste sour, like lemon juice. Bases taste soapy or bitter, like parsley. But you don't need to taste them to find out which is which. You can make an indicator solution that will show the presence of an acid or base by changing color.

DIFFICULTY: 💪💪💪   MESS-O-METER: 💥 💥 💥   TIME: 30 MINUTES

1. Place the cabbage and water in the blender. Put the lid firmly on the blender and blend at high speed for about 10 seconds. The blended cabbage will form a purple liquid.

2. Place the strainer over the bowl and pour the liquid from the blender into the strainer. Save the purple water in the bowl. That's your indicator solution. Discard the solids in the strainer.

3. Use a liquid measuring cup to pour ¼ cup (60 ml) of the indicator solution into each of the six cups or glasses. Set one aside—this will be your control, showing you what the indicator solution originally looked like throughout the experiment.

4. Pour the lemon juice into one of the remaining cups. Stir the mixture with a spoon. What happens? How long does it take for a change to happen? Write this information down in your science notebook.

5. Using the four remaining cups, complete step 4 for the honey, baking soda, sugar, and egg white, stirring with a clean spoon each time. Document your predictions and outcomes in your scientific notebook.

MYSTERY SOLVED! Red cabbage juice works as an acid-base indicator solution because red cabbage contains anthocyanin, a plant pigment that changes color when it is mixed with an acid or a base.

TAKE 2! Using the pH scale, at right, which measures how acidic or how basic something is, arrange the cups from the lowest to the highest pH. In your science notebook, label whether each item you tested was an acid, a base, or neutral.

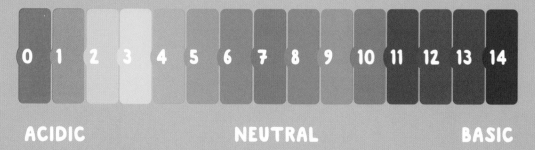

pH SCALE

| 0 | 1 | 2 | 3 | 4 | 5 | 6 | 7 | 8 | 9 | 10 | 11 | 12 | 13 | 14 |

ACIDIC   NEUTRAL   BASIC

All Puffed Up

Anyone who's roasted marshmallows over a campfire knows that they change as they heat up. What's happening to them, and why? Write your thoughts—or theories—in your science notebook, including how long you think it will take before a marshmallow starts to puff and how big you think it will get.

DIFFICULTY: ❤️❤️❤️   MESS-O-METER: ✹ ✹ ✹   TIME: 10 MINUTES

YOU WILL NEED

7 regular size marshmallows

Flexible measuring tape

3 paper plates

Microwave

Science notebook and pencil

1. Measure a marshmallow. How tall is it? How big is it around? (That's called the circumference.) Record this in your science notebook. Set the marshmallow aside—it's your control, for comparison.

2. Put two marshmallows on a paper plate, spaced far apart. Put the plate in the microwave. Cook for 30 seconds on HIGH.

3. Watch the marshmallows as they cook, and observe what happens to them. Write down any changes in your science notebook.

4. When the 30 seconds are up, remove the plate. Leave the hot marshmallows on the plate while you measure the height and circumference of each. Record the results in your science notebook.

5. Wait 30 more seconds to let the marshmallows cool slightly. Now taste one of them. Is it soft or crunchy?

6. Wait 2 more minutes. Did anything change in the other marshmallow? Now taste the other marshmallow. Did the size, taste, or texture change as it cooled off?

7. Repeat the experiment with two new marshmallows on a clean paper plate. This time heat them up for 45 seconds. What happened to them? Write down the results. Try it a third time, heating two new marshmallows up for 1 minute.

SAFETY TIP   If you overheat a marshmallow, it will explode—making a big sticky mess in the microwave and potentially burning anyone who touches it or tries to clean it up right away.

MYSTERY SOLVED! Marshmallows are made of sugar, water, gelatin, and a lot of air. Add heat from the microwave, and the water molecules move faster as they warm up, softening the sugar. It also warms the air molecules, which bounce around, expand, and push against the soft sugar walls, making the marshmallow puff up. When it cools down, the air bubbles deflate and the sugar hardens.

TAKE 2! Turn a marshmallow into a puffy pet by dipping a toothpick in a drop of food coloring on a paper plate. Draw eyes, ears, a mouth, perhaps whiskers. Then put it in the microwave for 30 to 45 seconds. What do you think will happen to the face? Or try polka dots. Will they get bigger when the marshmallow heats up? Will they grow farther apart or closer together? Use your imagination and have more marshmallow fun!

MARSHMALLOW CONCOCTIONS HAVE BEEN AROUND FOR MORE THAN 4,000 YEARS. ANCIENT EGYPTIANS USED THE SAP OF THE MARSH MALLOW PLANT TO TREAT SORE THROATS.

From Smell to Smile

Did you know that the flavors we taste when we eat are based more on how something smells than on how it tastes? Flavor starts when we inhale a food's aroma (how it smells), but it doesn't stop there. When we chew and swallow, odor from food molecules travels through our throat and into our nasal cavity. In fact, the flavors we experience are based about 80% on aroma and only 20% on how something tastes. In this experiment, let's find out what your nose knows by making three common kitchen combos that are used in very popular foods. Do you think you could tell which food item they represent just by sniffing?

DIFFICULTY: 💪💪💪 MESS-O-METER: 💥💥💥 TIME: 15 MINUTES

YOU WILL NEED

3 paper cups

Marker

Measuring spoons

Spice Combo 1

½ teaspoon each oregano, basil, onion powder, thyme, and garlic powder

Spice Combo 2

½ teaspoon each cumin, chili powder, garlic powder, onion powder, and oregano

Spice Combo 3

½ teaspoon each cinnamon, ginger, nutmeg, allspice, and cloves

Science notebook and pencil

1. Label each cup, 1 through 3.

2. In cup 1, measure out and combine the ingredients for Spice Combo 1.

3. In cup 2, measure out and combine the ingredients for Spice Combo 2.

4. In cup 3, measure out and combine the ingredients for Spice Combo 3.

5. Smell the contents of each cup, then record your thoughts in your science notebook. What does each combo smell like? What foods do you think of when you smell each? Do any stump you?

MYSTERY SOLVED! Spice Combo 1 is a common blend for pizza. Spice Combo 2 is often used for taco seasoning. Spice Combo 3 is common in baked goods like pumpkin pie, apple pie, and gingerbread.

TAKE 2! Sometimes an aroma sparks a memory or a feeling. That's because the front part of our brain, called the olfactory bulb, manages our sense of smell. It sends messages directly to the amygdala and the hippocampus, which are parts of the brain that are tied to emotion and memory. Try smelling the spice mixes again and see if they remind you of anything—a time or place—or make you feel a certain way. Write down your observations in your science notebook.

SPICE COMBO 1

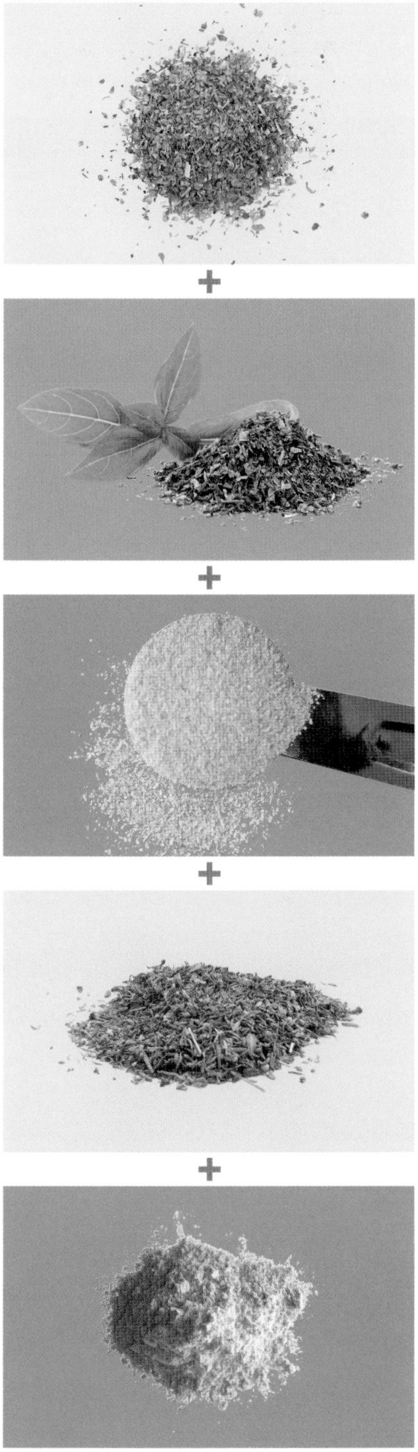

SPICE COMBO 2

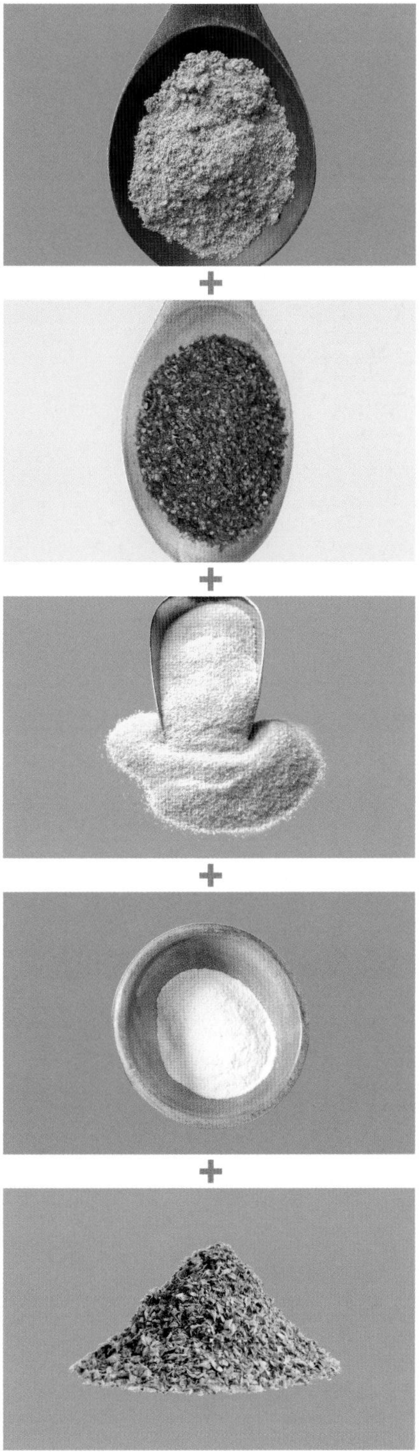

SPICE COMBO 3

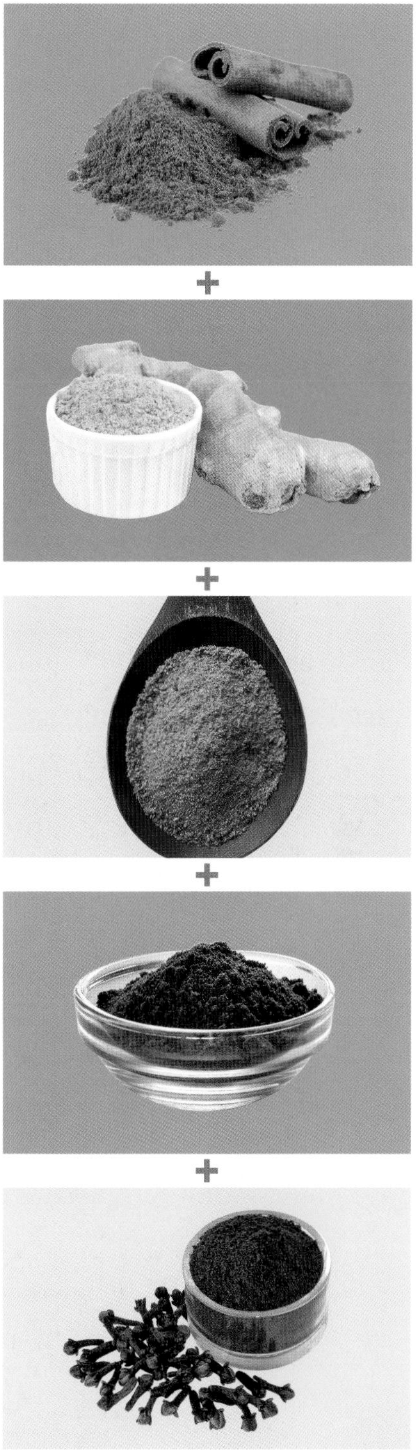

Odd Couples

Do you like salt on your French fries? How about sweet chocolate in a milkshake? What do you think about a salty milkshake or chocolaty fries? Though they might seem like opposites, there's actually a scientific reason why combining salty and sweet might be worth a try. Let's put this to the test.

DIFFICULTY: 💪💪💪   MESS-O-METER: ✺ ✺ ✺   TIME: 15 MINUTES

YOU WILL NEED

2 strawberries

1 pinch of salt

Small plate

2 apple slices

1 slice of cheddar cheese

1 fun-size chocolate bar (or square of chocolate candy bar)

1 salted pretzel

Science notebook and pencil

→ Ask an adult to cut the apple.

1. Eat a strawberry. How does it taste: sweet, sour, salty, bitter, or savory? Jot down your observations in your science notebook.

2. Sprinkle some salt on the plate and dip a strawberry into it, so you get a little bit of salt on the berry. Take a bite. How does this strawberry taste? Write down your observations.

3. Eat a slice of apple. How does it taste? Add your observations to your science notebook.

4. Add a slice of cheese to the top of the other apple slice and take a bite. How does the apple taste now? Write down your observations.

5. Take a bite of the chocolate. How does it taste? Jot down your observation.

6. Now eat the pretzel and a bite of chocolate together. Does the chocolate taste different? Write down your observations.

7. Which flavor combination was your favorite? Which one surprised you?

MYSTERY SOLVED! Chefs put salt on almost everything—and it's for a good reason. Salt enhances the flavor of foods. Your tongue seems to know this, too! Tongues have extra taste buds for sugar that activate only when salt is also present. And that's why salt makes things taste sweeter, not saltier.

TAKE 2! There are plenty of other interesting sweet and salty flavor combinations you can try. Here are just a few: avocado and fruit jam; potato chips and marshmallows; pickles and ice cream; watermelon and salt.

I HAVE 9,000 TASTE BUDS, AND DOGS HAVE ONLY 1,700.

BUT I HAVE SPECIAL TASTE BUDS FOR WATER. SLURRRRP!

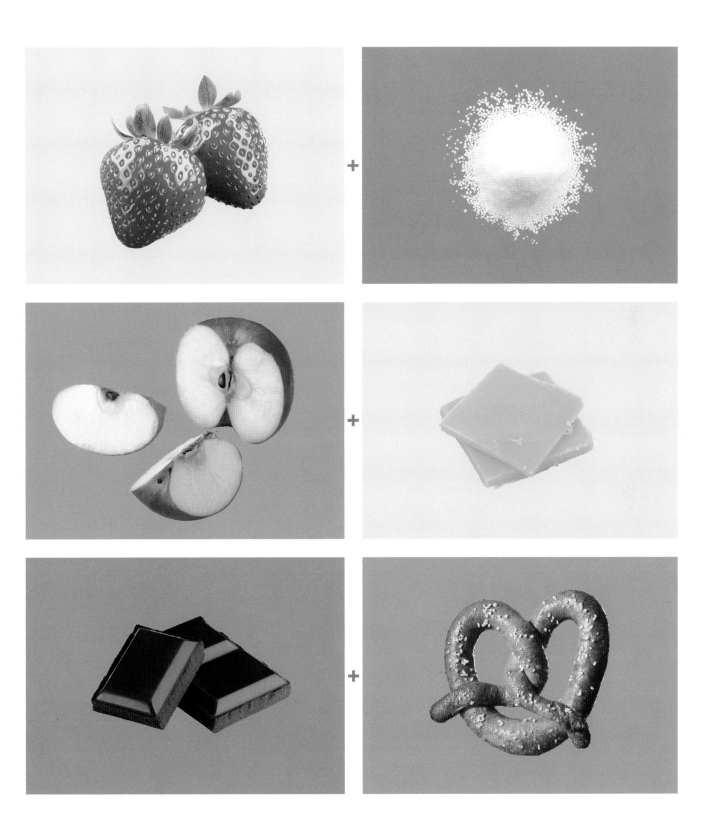

Taste It, Test It

The way you taste food is like a fingerprint—it's different for every person. Most people can detect the five basic tastes: sweet, sour, salty, bitter, and savory (which is sometimes called umami, the Japanese word for savory). Which tastes are your favorites? And how sensitive are you to each one? Find out by challenging your taste buds with this edible experiment.

DIFFICULTY: 💪💪💪   **MESS-O-METER:** ✹ ✹ ✹   **TIME: 30 MINUTES**

YOU WILL NEED

13 paper cups

Marker

Measuring spoons

1 tablespoon honey

1 tablespoon lemon juice

1 teaspoon salt

1 teaspoon unsweetened cocoa powder

1 tablespoon low-sodium soy sauce

Water

Science notebook and pencil

1 tablespoon plain yogurt

1 potato chip

1 piece of dark chocolate

1 tablespoon grated Parmesan cheese

1 leaf of kale

1 mushroom

1 piece of banana

1 cherry tomato

5 Popsicle sticks

1. Mark five paper cups with the Basic Tastes: Sweet, Sour, Salty, Bitter, and Savory. Mark the remaining cups with the numbers 1 through 8.

2. Put the honey in the Sweet cup, the lemon juice in the Sour cup, the salt in the Salty cup, the cocoa powder in the Bitter cup, and the soy sauce in the Savory cup. Add 1 tablespoon of water to the salt and stir to dissolve. Rinse the spoon and add 1 tablespoon of water to the cocoa and stir to dissolve. Rinse the spoon.

3. Make a chart like the one below in your science notebook. Put one type of food in each cup as described in the chart. For example, in the first cup, add plain yogurt. In the second one, add a potato chip, and so on.

TEST TASTE	SWEET	SOUR	SALTY	BITTER	SAVORY
CUP 1: PLAIN YOGURT					
CUP 2: POTATO CHIP					
CUP 3: DARK CHOCOLATE					
CUP 4: PARMESAN CHEESE					
CUP 5: KALE					
CUP 6: MUSHROOM					
CUP 7: BANANA					
CUP 8: TOMATO					

4. Try the Basic Tastes, using a different Popsicle stick for each.

5. Try the Test Taste in cup number 1. What Basic Taste is it most like? Place an X in that column. One by one, try each Test Taste and mark down your observations on the chart. Hint: Some Test Tastes may remind you of more than one Basic Taste.

MYSTERY SOLVED!
Most people taste similar flavors in similar ways: banana is sweet, yogurt is sour, potato chip is salty, kale is bitter, and mushroom is savory. Does this match how these foods tasted to you? Some foods convey more than one Basic Taste category: parmesan is savory and salty; tomato is savory, sweet, and sour; and dark chocolate is bitter and sweet. There's no right and wrong on this test. If you try this challenge with a friend or family member, you may find that you don't always agree. It's a matter of taste!

TAKE 2!
Hold your nose, then take a bite of one of the food items. Does it taste the same as before? Do you taste anything at all? Your sense of smell is very important to your ability to taste, and your brain needs both taste and smell to sense flavors. Try this with the other food items and record your responses again. How do they match with the results of your first taste tests?

GH NUTRITION LAB

OUR EXPERT SAYS

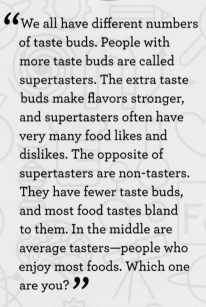

"We all have different numbers of taste buds. People with more taste buds are called supertasters. The extra taste buds make flavors stronger, and supertasters often have very many food likes and dislikes. The opposite of supertasters are non-tasters. They have fewer taste buds, and most food tastes bland to them. In the middle are average tasters—people who enjoy most foods. Which one are you?"

—Stefani Sassos
Registered Dietitian

FAB FACTS ABOUT FOOD

Two for the Row

Pick up an ear of corn and count the rows circling the cob. How many are there? A typical ear has 16 rows. And the number of rows will almost always be even. Corn kernels start as flowers. Each flower doubles as it grows, forming two rows. That adds up to an even number of rows, and even numbers are always divisible by two.

Flow or No?

Sir Isaac Newton thought that most liquids had a constant viscosity or flow. But that's not always the case. Ketchup is considered a non-Newtonian fluid. That means sometimes it acts more like a solid and sometimes it acts more like a liquid. It changes depending on how much force is applied to it. That's why when you thump hard on the bottom of a bottle of ketchup, it suddenly flows out quickly. Find out more about non-Newtonian fluids on pages 118 to 121.

Cookie Math

To make 9 sugar cookies, a recipe calls for 2½ cups flour, 1¼ cup sugar, and ½ teaspoon vanilla. If you want to double the recipe, how much flour, sugar, and vanilla will you need? How many cookies will you have at the end? If you eat ⅙ of the cookies, how many will be left?

(Answer: 5 cups flour, 2½ cups sugar, and 1 teaspoon vanilla. You'll have 18 cookies. One-sixth of 18 is 3; 18 minus 3 equals 15. That's enough to share with friends and family!)

Crunch Your Thirst

If you're thirsty you can grab a glass of water—or eat a cuke! Cucumbers and iceberg lettuce are 96% water. Zucchinis, tomatoes, and celery are also very high in water content—about 95% each.

Don't Bug Out!

There may be insects in your favorite red gummies (and lots of other red foods and beverages, too). Does the label include the ingredient carmine or cochineal extract? That's a dye made from crushed cochineal bugs. These insects live on cactus plants and eat the red cactus berries, which color their bodies.

Double Trouble

Drink some orange juice. Sweet and yummy, right? Brush your teeth and then take another sip. It probably won't taste good at all. That's because your taste buds are very sensitive. The ingredient that makes toothpaste foam (called sodium lauryl sulfate) can temporarily reduce our ability to taste sweetness and increase our ability to detect bitter flavors.

Blue Clue

Blue foods are very rare. But why? Plants are colored by a mix of natural pigments: carotenoids (orange, yellow, red), chlorophyll (green), and anthocyanins (blue, purple, and red). When these pigments mix, red wins out more often than blue. That's because red is present in both carotenoids and anthocyanins.

COLD AND HOT IN THE KITCHEN

We can change the way food looks, feels, and tastes by cooking it or cooling it. But fire and ice play an even more important role. Without heat, we wouldn't be able to easily make and eat the energy-filled meals we enjoy. And without ice, we wouldn't be able to keep our foods fresh for long. It turns out, the chemistry behind fire and ice has changed the course of human history.

Chill Things Down

How does liquid water change to its solid state, ice? When the molecules get cold, they slow down and expand. The colder the water gets, the more the molecules slow and expand. When the water reaches 32°F (0°C), they move so slowly that the molecules can hook onto each other and form a solid ice crystal.

    Cool (literally) fact: When the molecules expand, they also become less dense. That's why ice cubes float in a glass of water and icebergs float on the ocean.

Why Refrigeration?

If you leave an apple on the counter for two weeks, it will spoil. It will look puckered, soft, and brown, and may smell bad. But if you put that same apple in the refrigerator and pull it out one month later, it will look just fine. Why?

    Refrigeration slows down processes that make food spoil. Rotten food can make people sick. Cold temperatures slow the growth of mold and bacteria, and they also slow down the processes that make a fruit or vegetable ripen and decay. That's why a refrigerated apple ages more slowly. And that's a yummy fact!

NOT REFRIGERATED

REFRIGERATED

Turn Up the Heat

If water is heated, it will boil when it reaches 212°F (100°C). What causes this reaction? The energy from the heat source is transferred to the water molecules. All molecules are in motion all the time, and this heat-driven energy makes individual water molecules move more quickly. Some of the molecules form big bubbles. The bubbles are lighter than the water and rise to the surface, making the water boil. These water vapor bubbles form as liquid (water) changes to a gas (vapor). So a pot of boiling water is actually a pot of water that's in two different physical states—gas and liquid.

Fire Starter

To make the chemical reaction that makes a fire, it takes heat, fuel, and oxygen. Heat is what starts the fire, fuel is what feeds the flames, and oxygen keeps the flames burning.

Fire and Food

Before there were stoves, ovens, and microwaves, people cooked food over an open fire. They had to build and spark a fire every time they were hungry. That takes a lot of work! But cooking with fire was very important for the evolution of early humans.

About 2 million years ago, early humans began to grow taller, and their brains eventually doubled in size. Some scientists believe these changes were only possible when early humans started cooking with fire. Cooked food is easier to chew and easier for the body to digest. That means cooked food could give early humans more energy while requiring less work to process it.

Whirling Water

A vortex in water forms because of
something called centripetal force.
This force keeps the the water moving
in a curved path toward the center.
As gravity pulls the fluid downward,
it spins more quickly. Does it look like
a tornado? That's a vortex formed by
swirling air.

Chapter 2
WATER WORKS

Many interesting things happen when water is involved. Some objects float in it and others sink. Water can transform from liquid to gas, and the resulting steam fogs up the bathroom mirror. And while it flows in a straight stream from a faucet, water acts very differently when it drains from a sink or toilet. What's going on—and why? It turns out that the bathroom is full of chemistry, engineering, and yes, even math. You can't get clean without S.T.E.A.M.!

EXPERIMENTS

Spin Is In

There's a lot going on with the water in your bathroom. Look at the water in your toilet after you've flushed it. Then watch water in the sink or bathtub as it drains. Does the water go straight down or does it spin in a circular motion? Does it move the same way every time? Jot down your observations in your science notebook.

DIFFICULTY: 💪💪💪 **MESS-O-METER:** ✺ ✺ ✺ **TIME: 15 MINUTES**

YOU WILL NEED

1-liter soda bottle, empty, rinsed, label removed

Water

Sink or bathtub

Science notebook and pencil

1. Fill the soda bottle about three-quarters of the way to the top with water. Use one hand to hold it over a sink or bathtub. Place your other hand over the opening and turn the bottle upside down. Remove your hand and watch what happens inside the bottle as the water pours out. Did the water dribble out of the bottle, did it rush out, or did something else happen? Did it spin or not? Write down your observations in your science notebook.

2. Fill the soda bottle about three-quarters of the way to the top again. Put the cap back on the bottle. Swirl the water in the bottle in a clockwise motion by moving your arms in a circular motion in front of your body. Do this quickly, three times in a row. In what direction is the water moving inside the bottle? Is it moving in the same direction as the motion you made? What does the shape of the swirling water look like? Set the bottle down. Write down your observations.

3. Repeat step 2 but swirl the bottle three times in a counterclockwise motion. In which direction is the water moving—the same or the opposite direction as the motion you made? What is the shape of the water? Write down your observations.

4. Remove the cap. What do you think will happen if you place one hand over the opening of the bottle, turn the bottle upside down over the sink or tub, swirl the bottle, and then remove your hand? Write down your prediction. Give it a try and let the water run out immediately after swirling the bottle. Was your prediction correct?

SALTSTRAUMEN MAELSTROM IN NORWAY IS ONE OF THE WORLD'S MOST POWERFUL NATURAL WHIRLPOOLS.

IT SPINS UP TO 23 MILES PER HOUR. THAT'S 37 KILOMETERS PER HOUR.

MYSTERY SOLVED! You may have heard that water always swirls down a drain one way in the Northern Hemisphere and the opposite way in the Southern Hemisphere. But when it comes to toilets, the way the water swirls is about the toilet itself and how the plumbing works. Since water will swirl in whichever direction it is moved, the design of the toilet and the bathroom plumbing determine which way the water drains.

When a toilet is flushed, water enters the bowl from one side. That force creates a swirling motion, or a vortex, in the same direction every time it is flushed. Water in a bathtub sloshes (moves back and forth). The direction the water sloshes determines which way it drains when you pull the plug. When it comes to sinks, the shape of a sink (or the movement of your hands in the water) can determine which way the water will drain.

This is exactly what happens in this experiment. When you swirl the bottle, the water starts rotating in the same direction that your arms move the bottle—clockwise or counterclockwise. The force of your motion directs the way the water moves and how it runs out of the open bottle.

Fight the Fog

If you like taking steamy showers, then you're no stranger to a foggy mirror. It's hard to get ready if you can't see yourself. Instead of risking combing your nose or brushing your ear, try this experiment to see if you can resolve this steamy problem. Do you have any thoughts about why a mirror fogs up during a shower?

DIFFICULTY: 💪💪💪 **MESS-O-METER:** ✸ ✸ ✸ **TIME: 15 MINUTES**

YOU WILL NEED

You, ready for a shower

1 can shaving cream

Washcloth

Bathroom mirror

Shower

Science notebook and pencil

1. Spray shaving cream onto a washcloth and wipe it across the bottom half of a bathroom mirror. Rub it in completely so no shaving cream remains. Leave the top half of the mirror untouched. Do you think the shaving cream will affect whether or not the mirror fogs up during your shower? Jot down your prediction.

2. With the bathroom door closed, take a warm shower that lasts long enough to steam up the mirror. (About 5 minutes should be enough time.)

3. When you step out of the shower, check out the mirror. Does the top half, without the shaving cream, look the same as the bottom half? Does what happened match your prediction? Write down your observations.

4. Try wiping the fog from the mirror with your hand. What happens? If it changes, does the change last?

MYSTERY SOLVED!
When you take a shower, some of the warm water evaporates, becoming water vapor called steam. The steam warms the air in the bathroom. When the warm, moist air hits the cooler surface of the mirror, it turns back into a liquid. This transformation, called condensation, leaves tiny water droplets on the mirror. Water droplets are curved, and it's hard to see through a curved surface, making the top half of the mirror look foggy.

The bottom half of the mirror stays clear because of the shaving cream. It leaves an invisible coating that turns the individual curved droplets into a single, flat sheet of water that is easier to see through. Soap works in a similar way to keep glass from fogging up. In fact, this is such an annoying problem that you can buy professional defogging products for mirrors, glasses, and swim goggles, too.

TAKE 2! Can you think of another common personal care product that will work as well as the shaving cream to keep the mirror fog-free? Try smearing toothpaste on the top part of the mirror (the area you didn't cover with shaving cream), using a washcloth to rub it in completely. Does the toothpaste prevent the mirror from fogging up when you shower? How does it compare with the results of your experiment with the shaving cream?

NOTE IT! Steamy air can condense on any cool surface, including bathroom counters, shower tiles, and even the floor. When you turn off the shower, the warm and cool air temperatures balance out, and eventually the condensation will evaporate.

Sink or Float?

Boats come in all shapes and sizes, but they have one thing in common: they float! A hammer sinks, but if you put a hammer inside a boat, it still floats. Why do some things sink, while other ones float? In this experiment, you'll test the limits of a simple large boat with small cargo.

DIFFICULTY: 💪💪💪 MESS-O-METER: ✹ ✹ ✹ TIME: 20 MINUTES

YOU WILL NEED

Several small coins

1 piece of aluminum foil, about 8 inches (20 cm) square

Large plastic tub or sink filled about halfway with water

Science notebook and pencil

1. Hold a coin in one hand and the aluminum foil in the other. Which is heavier? Which is bigger? Write down your observations in your science notebook.

2. Make a prediction: What will happen when you set a coin on the surface of the water? What will happen when you set foil on the surface of the water?

3. Set a coin on the surface of the water. What happens? Write it down.

4. Set the foil on the surface of the water. What happens? Write it down.

5. Set the coin on the foil sheet. Be careful not to push the foil underneath the water's surface. What happens?

6. Remove the coin and set it aside. Take the piece of aluminum foil out of the water and fold the edges up to make 1-inch (2.5 cm) sides all around. (See images A and B.) Now you have a little boat! Set it on the water's surface and watch it float. (See image C.)

7. Place a coin in the foil boat. Does it stay afloat? Add more coins, one at a time. How many can you add before the little boat sinks? Does it matter where you place your coins on the boat? (See images D and E.)

MYSTERY SOLVED! When it comes to sinking and floating, weight is not the only factor that matters. It's all about density, which is how heavy something is for its size. A coin is denser than water—it's heavy for its small size—which is why it sinks. The aluminum foil is less dense than water, so it floats. It's lightweight for its larger size. As long as the boat and its cargo of coins are less dense than the water, they stay afloat.

TAKE 2! To hold more coins, the aluminum foil boat would have to be larger, longer, or wider. A bigger boat can handle more weight without sinking, as long as its density is still less than that of the water. Can you build a larger aluminum foil boat that can hold more coins? What happens if you make a longer, narrower boat—can it carry more or fewer coins?

IT TAKES ABOUT 90% LESS ENERGY TO RECYCLE AN ALUMINUM CAN THAN TO MAKE A NEW ONE. REUSE, REPURPOSE, RECYCLE!

B

D

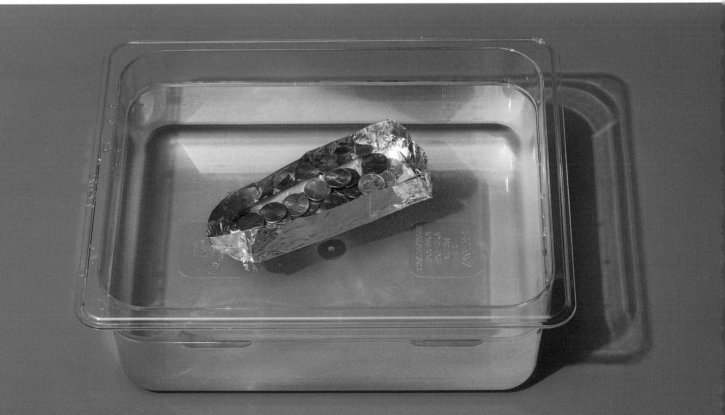

Giant Bubble Rainbows

A great time to spot a rainbow is after it rains and the sun comes out. You may also see a rainbow on a sunny day near a waterfall that's making especially big splashes. But you don't have to leave the house to spot a rainbow.

YOU WILL NEED

Spoon

½ cup (120 ml) bubble solution

Paper straw

Toilet paper or paper towel tube

Science notebook and pencil

→ Use store-bought bubbles or the recipe below.

DIFFICULTY: 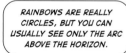 MESS-O-METER: TIME: 15 MINUTES

1. Pour three spoonfuls of bubble solution onto a smooth countertop in the bathroom or kitchen and spread it around.

2. Dip the straw into the container of bubble solution, place the soapy end of the straw on the soapy countertop, and blow a bubble. Then blow gently against it. What do you see? Are there colors on the bubble's surface? Record your observations.

3. Try the same thing using a toilet paper or paper towel tube instead of a straw to blow bubbles. Can you make a bigger bubble? Is it easier to see the rainbow of colors on a bigger bubble's surface? Write your observations in your science notebook.

MYSTERY SOLVED! Rainbows form when light beams are bent by water droplets. As the light beam passes through the water, it reflects (bends) and refracts (separates) into different wavelengths (colors). As bubbles float through the air, light beams shine through them and form mini rainbows.

RAINBOWS ARE REALLY CIRCLES, BUT YOU CAN USUALLY SEE ONLY THE ARC ABOVE THE HORIZON.

Make Your Own Bubble Solution
Pour **1 cup (240 ml) warm water** and **1 tablespoon sugar** into a small bowl and stir until the sugar is completely dissolved. Then add **2 tablespoons dish soap** and stir the ingredients together gently. If you have more bubble mix than you need for this experiment, you can store it in a clean covered jar or container for up to 2 weeks.

Bubble Buddies

When you blow bubbles, some float off into the air, others land with a splat, and some meet up midflight. Why do they come together? Try this double-bubble experiment to find out.

YOU WILL NEED

1 spoon

½ (120 ml) cup bubble solution

3 paper straws (you only need 1, but they can get soggy, so plan to have backups)

Science notebook and pencil

→ Use store-bought bubbles or the recipe on page 50.

1. First, pour three spoonfuls of bubble solution onto a smooth countertop in the bathroom or kitchen and spread it around.

2. Dip the straw into the container of bubble solution, place the soapy end of the straw on the soapy countertop, and blow a bubble. If the bubble pops too quickly or doesn't form, add another spoonful of bubble solution to the countertop. What shape is the bubble? Did you make a big bubble or a small one? Write down your observations in your science notebook.

3. Blow a second bubble next to the first one. (If it pops, blow another one. You need two bubbles next to each other for this step.) Blow on the second bubble so that it moves toward the first bubble. What happens? Write it down.

4. Blow four more bubbles near one another until you've formed a cluster of bubbles. What does the cluster look like? What shape is it? Write down your observations, and draw a picture, too.

MYSTERY SOLVED!

A bubble is a sphere, which is a perfectly round and symmetrical geometric shape. Something is symmetrical when you can fold it in half and both halves have the same shape. This shape allows a bubble to contain the most air while taking up the least amount of surface area. This is also why bubbles are attracted to one another. Even when their shape is already efficient (using less energy), they're still looking for ways to reduce their surface area. When they get near each other, they connect and share a wall, making them more efficient.

THE RECORD FOR THE MOST PEOPLE TO FIT INSIDE A SOAP BUBBLE IS 417.

TAKE 2! Is there a way to blow a bubble within a bubble? Try blowing one large bubble on the soapy surface. Now dip your straw in the bubble solution (make sure the outside of the straw is coated in bubble solution) and slowly insert it into the large bubble. (This may take a few tries. If your bubble pops, cover your straw with more bubble solution and try again.) Once you've inserted the straw into the bubble successfully, blow a second, smaller bubble inside the larger bubble. Make sure it doesn't get too big or the bubbles will merge. How many bubbles-within-a-bubble can you blow before they stick together?

NOTE IT! When two bubbles meet, they not only attach to each other, but they change shape, too. Once connected, they share a flat wall. If many bubbles stick together, they resemble beehive cells, also hexagons.

Thicker Picker-Uppers

In every bathroom you'll find a roll of toilet paper. But why toilet paper and not a piece of tissue? Or a paper towel? They're all paper, and they're often designed to be thrown away after one use. But some paper products are stronger, some disintegrate quickly, and others are more absorbent. In this experiment, you will test three types of paper and determine what properties make them perfect for the job they have to do.

Which paper product do you think will be the strongest when it gets wet, and which will be the weakest? Why might they have been designed that way? Write your predictions in your science notebook.

DIFFICULTY: 💪💪💪   **MESS-O-METER:** ✸ ✸ ✸   **TIME: 30 MINUTES**

YOU WILL NEED

Science notebook and pencil

1 to 3 pieces of toilet paper (enough to cover the top of a paper cup)

1 facial tissue

1 paper towel sheet

3 paper cups

3 rubber bands

Measuring spoons

1 cup water

Several small coins

1. In your science notebook, make a chart like the one below.

TYPE OF PAPER	NUMBER OF TEASPOONS (ABSORBENCY)	NUMBER OF COINS (STRENGTH)
TOILET PAPER		
FACIAL TISSUE		
PAPER TOWEL		

2. Place the toilet paper on top of the first cup and secure it with a rubber band. Place the facial tissue on top of the second cup and secure it with a rubber band. Place the paper towel on top of the third cup and secure it with a rubber band.

3. Starting with the toilet paper–covered cup, pour 1 teaspoon of water onto the center of the toilet paper. Observe what happens. Add another teaspoon of water. Then a third teaspoon. Does the toilet paper absorb the water or break?

4. If the paper held up, place a coin on top of the wet area. Then add another. How many coins are you able to add before it breaks? Record the results on your chart.

5. Repeat steps 3 and 4 with the facial tissue–covered cup and record the results on your chart.

6. Repeat steps 3 and 4 with the paper towel–covered cup and add the results to your chart.

MYSTERY SOLVED!

The sheets of toilet paper, facial tissue, and paper towel absorb liquids because they are made from trees or bamboo. These plants contain cellulose, which is made up of sugar molecules. Water molecules are attracted to sugar molecules, and that's how they absorb water. Sweet!

But these three different paper products were engineered for three different purposes. Toilet paper is designed to disintegrate quickly in water so that it doesn't clog the sewer systems. It's the only paper product that can be safely flushed. How did it score in absorbency and strength?

Facial tissue needs to remain intact when you sneeze or blow your nose. It needs to be strong enough that it doesn't disintegrate when it gets wet. How did the facial tissue score compared to the toilet paper and paper towels?

Paper towels are designed to clean up a mess. They need to soak up and hold a lot of liquid without breaking apart. How did paper towels score in comparison to the other paper items?

OUR EXPERT SAYS

GH TEXTILES LAB

" We test toilet paper softness three ways. First, testers come into the lab and rate the softness in a blind comparison. Next, testers use the toilet paper in bathrooms for additional ratings, to see how it feels during use. Finally, a special machine that mimics what your hand feels when it touches the paper gives a computerized softness score. We combine these softness tests with strength and dissolvability tests to find the best toilet paper. "

—Lexie Sachs
**Textiles Director,
Good Housekeeping Institute**

Floating Fish

What if you could draw your own fish and then watch it come to life? It sounds impossible, right? With the help of some dry erase markers, you can test this idea and find out. What do you think will happen if you combine water and a doodle made from dry erase ink? Write down your prediction in your science notebook.

DIFFICULTY: 💪💪💪 **MESS-O-METER:** ✸ ✸ ✸ **TIME: 15 MINUTES**

1. Draw the outline of a fish on the bottom of the plate or tray. Retrace your drawing to make sure all the lines are connected. Let dry for a minute or two.

2. Fill the measuring cup with tap water. Place the pour spout just inside the corner of the dish and add water very slowly until it just covers the bottom. Be careful not to pour water directly onto your drawing or make splashes near it. The water will move toward your drawing, eventually surrounding it. Observe what happens and jot it down in your science notebook. If the water splashes or it doesn't work on your first try, empty the dish, erase the drawing with a paper towel, dry off the dish, and try again.

3. Tilt the dish slightly from side to side. What happens? Jot it down.

MYSTERY SOLVED!
The ink in dry erase markers is engineered to be slippery. It's made with a chemical that causes it to easily release from surfaces. (Permanent markers are made with a chemical that makes the ink stick to surfaces, so be sure not to use these in your experiment!)

The easy-release ink lets go from a surface, but why does it float? There are two reasons. First, dry erase ink isn't soluble, which means it won't dissolve in water. Second, dry erase ink is less dense than the water, so it becomes buoyant, meaning it can float. When you tilt the dish, the fish moves around on the water's surface.

TAKE 2!
Pour out the water and begin again. What other doodles can you bring to life with water and dry erase ink? Try a starfish, a dolphin, a mermaid, or an eel. Do they all work well? Does shape matter? What about size?

ONE DROP OF WATER CONTAINS ABOUT 1,500,000,000,000,000,000,000 MOLECULES.

THAT'S 1.5 SEXTILLION.

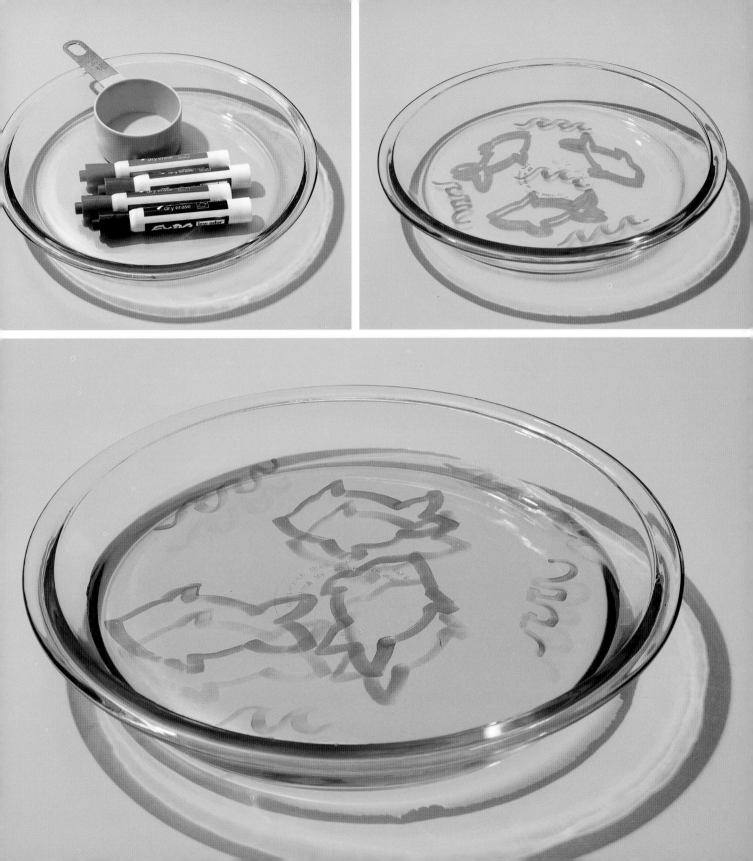

FAB FACTS ABOUT WATER

Watch Out!

There's an invisible vortex in your bathroom and it's called a toilet plume. It forms when a toilet is flushed and droplets spin into the air above it. This means some of what was in the toilet is now floating around in the air landing on your toothbrush, and settling onto your hair. Ick! So here's a tip: Keep the lid down when you flush! (For some vortex fun, check out **Spin Is In on page 44**.)

Vortices (the plural of vortex) happen outside of the bathroom, too. Tornadoes, galaxies, and whirlpools are just a few examples of vortices in nature.

Pee-ew!

Asparagus contains a substance called asparagusic acid. When our bodies break it down, it turns into sulfur-containing molecules. That's what gives urine a strong smell after a person eats asparagus. Sulfur is what makes skunk spray stink, too. The same chemical in garlic that makes your breath smell can also make your pee smell.

Poop Producers

The average human in the U.S. makes more than 300 pounds (136 kg) of poop per year, which adds up to 25,000 pounds (11,340 kg) over a lifetime. That's about as heavy as two *Tyrannosaurus rexes*.

Round and Round

Water is constantly moving from Earth's surface to the atmosphere and back again. The sun's heat evaporates liquid water on Earth into water vapor. The gas rises into the cool atmosphere, where it condenses into water droplets (clouds). Heavy clouds drop precipitation that seeps into the ground or flows into oceans, lakes, and rivers. Then the water cycle starts again.

Reduce Your Use

Water runs out of a typical sink faucet at 1 gallon (3.8L) per minute, and 2 to 5 gallons (7.5L to 19L) per minute in the shower. You can save water by turning it off while you brush your teeth and by taking short showers.

Watery Planet

About 71% of Earth's surface is covered with water. Most of that water (96.5%) is in the oceans. The remaining 3.5% is fresh water that is mostly frozen as polar ice caps and glaciers.

Bright Light

Nearly a century and a half ago, Thomas Edison invented the first light bulb that was inexpensive and long-lasting. In an incandescent bulb, also called an Edison bulb, electricity heats a metal filament (wire) that glows. *Incandescent* means emitting light from heat.

Chapter 3

POWER UP!

Energy revs up our daily lives. While you may not see it buzzing in the background, it powers our lights, computers, heat and air conditioning, kitchen appliances, school buses, and cars. Understanding how it works gives us power, too—to build better technology and a healthier planet. Turn the page to start learning about the energy we get from motors, light, electricity, and more.

Battery Blast

Can you imagine your life without batteries? They provide electrical energy whenever we need it—no cord required. Without batteries, we wouldn't have portable electronic devices such as phones, computers, and remote controls. How do batteries work? Let's find out.

DIFFICULTY: 💪💪💪 **MESS-O-METER:** ☀ ☀ ☀ **TIME: 30 MINUTES**

YOU WILL NEED

Graphite art pencil (grade 6B or higher)

2 pieces of smooth white paper

Ruler

2 mini (5 mm) light-emitting diode (LED) bulbs

Needle-nose pliers

Tape

2 9-volt batteries

Science notebook and pencil

→ When using these in Step 3, ask an adult to help.

1. Using the pencil, draw the shape of a flashlight on a piece of paper. It should be about 2 inches (5 cm) long. Leave a small gap (no more than ¼ inch/6.5 mm) in the middle of the short ends of your drawing. On the left side of each gap, write a positive (+) sign and the right side, make a negative (-) sign. This is your flashlight. Go over your lines three to five times—for the experiment to work best, they need to be dark and thick. (See the photo on page 64.)

2. Look at the mini LED bulbs. Each has two legs (wires) sticking out. One leg is longer than the other. The longer end is the positive (+) end, and the shorter end is the negative (-) end.

3. Using the needle-nose pliers, carefully bend the legs of each bulb outward 90 degrees (making an L shape) at the halfway point. Set one bulb aside.

4. Place the LED bulb upright in the gap at one end of your flashlight, positioning it so the ends of the bent legs touch the pencil line. The positive (longer) leg should touch the positive side, and the negative (shorter) leg should touch the negative side of the gap. Tape the legs in place. Observe your drawing. Is the light glowing?

5. Look at the battery. There are two electrodes (small bumps on top where electric current enters or leaves the battery). Observe that one is labeled + (positive) and one is labeled – (negative).

6. Place the battery upside down, centered on the gap at the other end of your flashlight. (The electrodes will be touching the paper.) Position it so that the positive electrode touches the line nearest the + sign and the negative electrode touches the line nearest the - sign. What happened when you attached the battery to the pencil line? Record your observation in your science notebook. Remove the battery to continue with the experiment.

7. On the second sheet of paper, draw a flashlight that's twice as long as the first one—about 4 inches (10 cm). Leave a small gap (no more than ¼ inch/6.5 mm) in the middle of the short ends of your drawing, exactly as you did with the smaller flashlight.

8. Tape the legs of the second bulb to the gap in the top of the flashlight, arranging them the same way you did in step 4.

9. Now attach the battery to the gap in the bottom of the flashlight shape, arranging it the same way you did in step 6. What happened? Record your observation in your science notebook.

10. Place the battery back on your shorter flashlight and compare the shorter and longer flashlights. Are they the same? Is one bulb brighter than the other? Write your observations in your science notebook. Remove the batteries from your flashlights when you're finished with the experiment.

CONTINUED

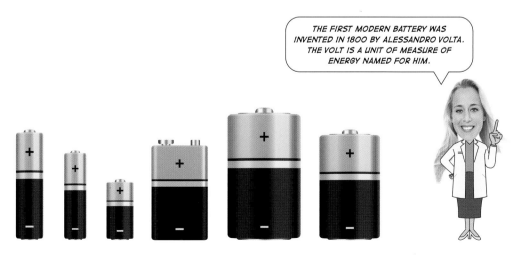

THE FIRST MODERN BATTERY WAS INVENTED IN 1800 BY ALESSANDRO VOLTA. THE VOLT IS A UNIT OF MEASURE OF ENERGY NAMED FOR HIM.

MYSTERY SOLVED! Graphite is an electrical conductor. That means electricity can easily pass through it. But conductors can't do anything on their own. And neither can batteries. It takes teamwork to make electricity.

Batteries store chemical energy. They convert it into electrical energy (electricity) when there is a flow of electrons from the positive electrode to the negative electrode. The conductor—in this case the graphite pencil drawing—gives the electrons a path along which they can flow.

The electrical current runs out from the positive electrode of the battery through the graphite path and into the positive electrode of the light bulb. It continues on through the negative electrode of the light bulb, back onto the graphite path, and into the negative electrode of the battery. This flow of electricity is a closed circuit. In a closed circuit, electrons flow continuously without being interrupted.

Electric current needs a closed circuit to travel through. When you attached the light to the paper, it didn't turn on. When you added a power source—the battery—the circuit was closed and electrons could flow. In the larger flashlight, the bulb glows more dimly because the path the electrons travel is longer. The farther the light is from the battery, the less brightly the light will glow.

TAKE 2! Can you make a flashlight with a different shape? Try a circle—as long as you leave the same gaps at the top and bottom, can you create a closed circuit and make the light glow? What about a triangle? That might take a little more creative thinking, but give it a try!

GH
ENGINEERING
& TECH LAB

OUR EXPERT SAYS

"While single-use alkaline batteries (such as ones that you might have in your remotes) can go in the trash everywhere except California, it's more eco-friendly and safe to recycle them. Rechargeable batteries (such as those in cellphones) should not be put in the trash, as they may contain hazardous chemicals. To find out where and how to safely recycle all types of batteries, check call2recycle.org."

—Rachel Rothman
Chief Technologist & Director of Engineering

Light Energy

Light is made up of different wavelengths. We can see some light wavelengths as colors if we separate them from one another. This experiment is designed for a sunny day, but it will also work with a flashlight.

 DIFFICULTY: MESS-O-METER: TIME: 15 MINUTES

YOU WILL NEED

1 sheet white paper

Clear, smooth-sided glass filled to the top with water

Science notebook and pencil

1. Set the sheet of white paper near a window on a bright sunny day. Place the glass of water just behind it. What happens when the sunlight shines through the water and onto the paper? Make an observation in your notebook.

2. Adjust the position of the glass until the sunlight is streaming through the surface of the water, through the glass, and onto the paper in front of the glass. What happens to the light when it hits the paper? Record your observations in your notebook.

NOTE IT! You may need to move the glass around to capture the sun's rays at the right angle to make a rainbow on the paper.

MYSTERY SOLVED! Light is the only form of energy that we can see with our eyes. Visible light comprises different wavelengths (the distance between each wave), and each wavelength is represented with its own color. Violet light has the shortest wavelength, while red light has the longest wavelength.

White light is a combination of all the wavelengths on the visible spectrum. When the sunlight passes through the glass of water, it reflects (bounces off) the water droplets and refracts (bends), or changes direction. Because the colors travel at varying speeds, they bend at different angles. This causes them to separate.

TAKE 2! Try this experiment again with a small handheld flashlight in a darkened room or closet. Move the flashlight around: closer to the glass of water, farther away, and then at various angles. How does this change the colors you see in the light rays? How does the rainbow made from artificial light (the flashlight) compare to the rainbow created by the natural light (the sun)?

SUNLIGHT TRAVELS TO EARTH IN ABOUT 8 MINUTES AND 20 SECONDS.

Solar S'mores

Can you think of a way to make s'mores without a microwave or campfire? There's another source of energy you can use to make this ooey-gooey treat: the sun! How can the sun be used to cook food? You're about to find out! You're going to make your own solar oven.

DIFFICULTY: 💪💪💪 MESS-O-METER: ☀ ☀ ☀ TIME: 30 MINUTES HANDS-ON; 90-PLUS MINUTES TOTAL

YOU WILL NEED

For the oven

1 empty pizza box

Ruler

Pencil

Scissors

Aluminum foil

Tape

Plastic kitchen wrap

Black construction paper

Science notebook

For each s'more

2 graham cracker squares

1 marshmallow

1 piece of chocolate candy bar

→ Some of the cuts in this experiment are a little difficult, so ask an adult for help.

1. With the pizza box closed, use a ruler to measure 2 inches (5 cm) from each edge of the lid, and mark that distance with a pencil. (See image A.) Use the marks to draw a square on the top of the pizza box.

2. Ask an adult to help you cut along three sides of the square to create a flap. (Don't cut the side closest to the edge that connects to the bottom of the box.)

3. Fold the flap upward, making a crease in the uncut edge of the flap. Cover the inside of the flap with aluminum foil, shiny side facing out. Keep the foil as smooth as possible. Use tape to secure the foil to the top of the flap. (See image B.)

4. Open the lid completely and cover the inside of the window with two sheets of plastic wrap (a double layer). Pull taut, then secure both layers to the inside of the box, running tape along all of the edges to make a tight seal.

5. Open the entire lid and place a sheet of black construction paper on the bottom of the box. This will be your cooking surface.

6. Place two graham crackers on the black paper, about 1 inch (2.5 cm) apart. Place a marshmallow on one piece and a square of chocolate on the other. (See image C.)

7. Close the lid and prop open the aluminum foil flap with the ruler. (See image D.) Now your solar oven is ready!

CONTINUED

68

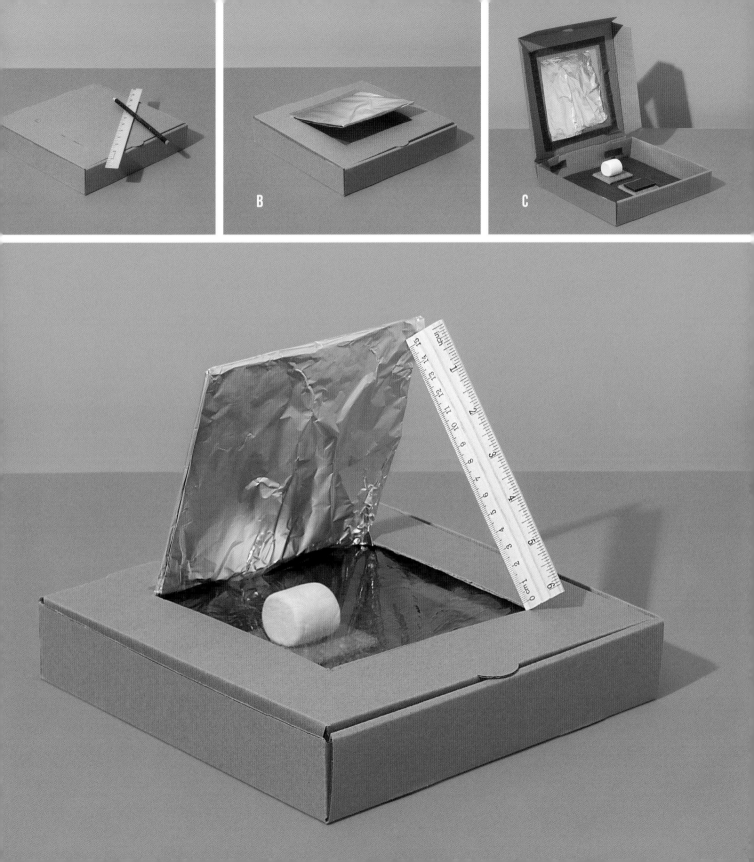

8. Set the box in a sunny spot. The goal is to get as much sunlight as possible to reflect off the foil-lined flap and into the box. Adjust the position of the box and the angle of the flap by adjusting the position of the ruler, if needed. Secure it by taping the ruler in place. In your science notebook, note the time that your solar oven is set up. How long do you think it will take for the chocolate and marshmallow to melt? Jot down your prediction.

9. Check on your s'more in 15 minutes: Peer through the plastic wrap, but don't open the lid. Check back again in another 15 minutes. Record the time and your observations.

10. Keep checking until the marshmallow and chocolate have melted. How long did it take? To finish your project, create a sandwich with the graham crackers and enjoy. That's some tasty science!

NOTE IT! Sunlight is usually strongest from 11 a.m. to 3 p.m., which makes this the best time for your experiment.

MYSTERY SOLVED! Solar ovens use the light and heat emitted by the sun. The sunlight reflects, or bounces off, the aluminum foil flap and is directed onto the black paper on the bottom of the pizza box. The color black retains heat, making it a good choice for a cooking surface. The plastic wrap traps heat inside the box, warming the air.

TAKE 2! Can you make your solar oven warm up faster? Try lining the inside of the box with aluminum foil (without covering the black cooking surface or the plastic window). Place new s'more ingredients inside and conduct the experiment again. Does the foil lining inside the box increase or decrease the cooking time?

Positivity Project

Can you generate electricity out of thin air? Yes! When you rub a balloon against your clothes and then stick it to a wall, you create static electricity. The same effect is at work when you take off a hat and your hair stands on end. Can this hair-raising reaction help you power a light bulb without screwing it into a lamp?

YOU WILL NEED

Inflated balloon

Compact fluorescent light bulb (CFL)

Science notebook and pencil

1. Sit in a dark room with the lights turned off. (This experiment needs to be conducted in these conditions for the best results!) Hold the light bulb in one hand and the balloon in your other hand.

2. Rub the balloon on your hair for 15 seconds. Make sure you move it around to rub all sides.

3. Now place the balloon close to the bottom of the light bulb. What happens?

4. Move the balloon closer and farther away from the bulb. What happens? Try moving the balloon up and down near the bulb. Does anything change? Write down your observations.

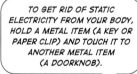

TO GET RID OF STATIC ELECTRICITY FROM YOUR BODY, HOLD A METAL ITEM (A KEY OR PAPER CLIP) AND TOUCH IT TO ANOTHER METAL ITEM (A DOORKNOB).

MYSTERY SOLVED! Everything in the universe is made up of atoms, and atoms are made of three main things: electrons, protons, and neutrons. Electricity is created when electrons move from one atom to another. When you rubbed the balloon on your hair, you charged it by transferring electrons from your hair to the balloon. When you placed the balloon near the light bulb, the negative charges jumped from the balloon to the bulb. And that gave the light bulb the spark of electricity. This is called static electricity.

What is it about CFL bulbs that make this experiment work? The inside of a CFL bulb is coated with a substance that contains phosphors, which emit light when they come in contact with energy—usually electrical current. In this experiment, the negatively charged balloon provides the spark to get the phosphors to glow.

TAKE 2! Try this experiment with a metal spoon and a balloon. Rub the balloon on your hair for 15 seconds, then place it close to the spoon. What happens?

ENERGY FROM NATURE

Winds blow, water flows, and the sun shines around the world every day. These are natural resources that can be used to make renewable energy—unending sources of power that put less strain on Earth's other, more limited resources.

Wind Power

Wind power can be harnessed by turbines. They look like very tall, skinny windmills. Why are they so tall? It's generally windier at higher heights, and the faster the wind blows, the more electricity the windmills can make. Strong winds spin blades around a rotor (like an airplane propeller). The rotor spins a shaft, sending energy to the generator, which creates electricity.

Unlike a fan, which uses electricity to make wind, turbines use wind to make electricity.

Hydropower

When flowing water spins a wheel, it is an example of generating hydropower. (*Hydro* means water in Greek). It is one of the oldest energy sources, and it's still widely used today. More than 70% of Washington State's electricity is powered by water.

Creating electricity from water can be done with turbines, machines with rotating blades that capture energy from moving liquid (or air). The force of the water rotates the turbine's blades. The blades are connected to a generator, which converts energy into electricity.

Hydropower can be generated from simple machines, like a waterwheel at a grist mill, or complex machines, like the dozens of massive turbines at the Grand Coulee Dam in Washington State. They turn kinetic energy (energy of movement) into electrical energy.

Solar Power

One way to harness the power of the sun is to use massive photovoltaic (PV) panels to convert sunlight into electrical energy. (*Photo* means light in Greek.) The PV panels often contain silicon, a common semiconductor used in computer chips and other electronic devices. When sunlight hits the silicon, electrons inside the silicon begin to move, creating electricity.

Solar energy can power electrical systems in homes, schools, and businesses, or supply local or national power needs. It can also be stored for use at another time. To harness your own solar power, try the **Solar S'mores experiment on page 68.**

The Grand Coulee Dam, on the Columbia River, is the largest hydroelectric power plant in the U.S. Located in Washington State, it generates enough electricity for more than 4 million homes.

FAB FACTS ABOUT ENERGY

Tall Order

When it comes to harvesting wind power, bigger is better: longer blades and taller turbines create more energy. The median height of a wind turbine built on land is about 499 feet (152 m), and the tallest offshore (built at sea) turbine under construction is 853 feet (260 m). The blades can be longer than a football field!

Statue of Liberty
(305 feet/93 m)

Haliade-X
(853 feet/260 m)

Eiffel Tower
(1,063 feet/324 m)

Empire State Building
(1,454 feet/443 m)

Stay and Play

If someone says you have a lot of energy, it probably means you're very active. Energy in motion is called kinetic energy. But energy exists even without movement. A ball on a table has potential energy—stored energy that can be used at a later time (such as if someone bumps into the table and the ball starts moving). So if you're told you're being lazy when you're lounging on the sofa, just say you're actively storing energy!

Star Power

The sun is not only the largest star in our solar system; it is the greatest renewable energy resource we have. Just an hour and a half of the planet's daily sunlight could provide enough energy to meet worldwide power usage for a full year, according to the U.S. Energy Department.

No plug? No problem!

Solar ovens are used to cook and boil water in places where electricity isn't always available. They are a safer and cleaner form of energy than open fires, and they're lightweight and portable. Plus, they cost nothing to power up—sunlight is free. To make your own, see **Solar S'mores (page 68)**.

That's Fan-tastic!

When you turn on a ceiling fan, it instantly cools a room, right? Not necessarily. Ceiling fans can actually help you stay warm in the winter. Most ceiling fans have a switch that will change the direction the blades spin. The blades can rotate counterclockwise, which blows air down and helps cool the room. But the blades can also spin clockwise. In the winter, this will help pull cold air upward and keep the warmer air at ground level.

Summer Mode

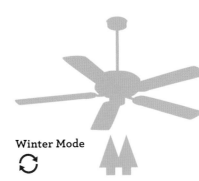

Winter Mode

Power Down

There are vampires in your home! Electronic appliances and devices are called vampires when they use power when turned off or in standby mode. They suck out electricity even when they're not in use. These include cable boxes, modems, computers, printers, game consoles, and phone chargers. To be a vampire slayer, you have to interrupt their connection to a power source. Plug your devices into a power strip, then turn off the power strip when you're not using them.

Sound Bite

Sound is a continuously vibrating wave that can travel through liquids, solids, and gases like air and plasma (used in neon signs). The speed at which sound waves move up and down is called frequency. This determines pitch—how high or low a sound is. Their height, called amplitude, determines volume, or loudness.

Chapter 4
ALL THE RIGHT MOVES

What do blowing a bubble, listening to music, and kicking a soccer ball have in common? Motion! There are forces all around us that make things move. Sometimes our own body—like our muscles or our breath—can help direct movement. Other times there are forces out of our control, like gravity, that impact movement. When they do impact movement, we can rely on physics (the science of matter and energy) to guide motion a certain way. Walk this way to learn more!

Wheel Fun

How can we move objects that are too heavy to lift and carry? There's a contraption on a tow truck that makes it easy to load a 4,000-pound (1,814-kg) car onto an inclined platform. It uses a few of the simple machines introduced on page 20. Try this experiment and learn how these simple machines work together.

DIFFICULTY: ❤❤❤ MESS-O-METER: ✸ ✸ ✸ TIME: 20 MINUTES

YOU WILL NEED

2 paper towel tubes

Scissors

Small piece of cardboard, at least 5-by-10 inches (13-by-25 cm)

Tape

2 pencils (one for writing and one for your machine)

Yarn or string

Ruler

Paper clip

Small, lightweight action figure or similar toy

Science notebook

> WINCHES ARE OFTEN USED IN THEATERS TO MOVE SCENERY ON AND OFF A STAGE.

1. Cut a ½-inch-deep (13-mm) V-shaped cutout into the opposite sides on one end of each paper towel tube. (See image A.) The cutouts should be wide enough that you can rest your pencil in them.

2. Place the small piece of cardboard flat on the floor. Place the tubes, V-shaped cutouts up, on the cardboard, about 3 inches (8 cm) apart. Tape the bottoms of the tubes to the cardboard so they stand straight up. (See image B.) Place the pencil in the cutouts.

3. Cut a 20-inch (51-cm) piece of yarn. Use tape to secure one end to the middle of the pencil. Wrap the yarn around the pencil. (See image C.)

4. Unbend the outside end of a paper clip and insert it into the pencil's eraser so the loop is sticking out. This will be your handle. (See image C.)

5. Twist the handle and observe what happens. Twist the handle the opposite way and observe. Write down the results in your science notebook.

6. Now tie the loose end of the yarn in a knot around your action figure. Turn the handle. (See image D.) What happens? Write down the results in your science notebook.

MYSTERY SOLVED! You made a hand-crank winch, a machine that makes moving heavy objects easier. It used an axle (the rotating pencil) and rope (the string) and a lever (the paper clip handle).

The axle and rope help redistribute the weight of the object (your action figure), which means you need less effort to lift it. Winches can lift things up, as you've seen, but they are often used to move something horizontally along a slight incline—such as pulling a car up onto a tow truck ramp or lowering a boat down a ramp into the water. To lift heavy loads up a steeper incline, or vertically (straight up), a hoist is used more often than a winch. A hoist has a mechanical braking system that can better handle vertical lifts of heavier loads.

TAKE 2! What if you have several things you want to carry up and down the winch, like a bunch of paper clips or marbles or several action figures? Can you design a reusable bucket or platform to carry all your stuff at once, so you don't have to lift the items one at a time? You may need extra materials, like a paper cup or other container. Sketch your idea in your science notebook, then give it a try.

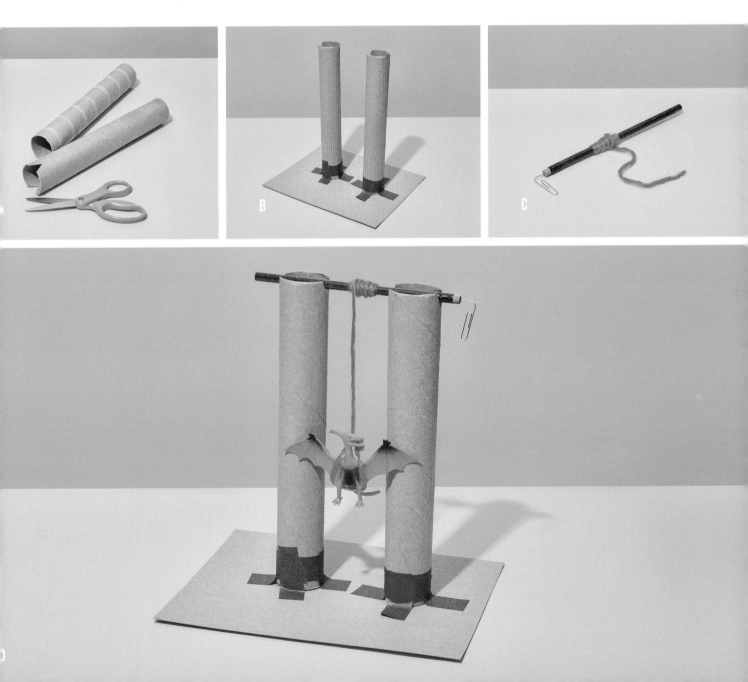

Blast Off

A soccer player kicks a ball. It flies through the air until—bam!—it hits the goalpost and bounces off. It rolls onto the grass and eventually comes to a stop. This is science in action. Make a prediction in your science notebook: What makes an object move? And what makes an object stop?

YOU WILL NEED

1 balloon

Scissors

1 toilet paper tube

Duct tape

Flexible measuring tape

3 pom-poms (or marshmallows)

Science notebook and pencil

DIFFICULTY: 💪💪💪   **MESS-O-METER:** ✺ ✺ ✺   **TIME: 20 MINUTES**

1. Knot the end of a deflated balloon. Cut ½ inch (13 mm) off the top.

2. Stretch the balloon over one end of the toilet paper tube. Secure the balloon with duct tape. Wrap the tube with duct tape to keep it stiff.

3. Stretch out the measuring tape so it's a few feet long and set it on the floor.

4. Sit down on the floor at the beginning of the measuring tape. Set a pom-pom on the floor in front of you, next to the measuring tape. Observe what happens. Did the pom-pom move?

5. Now drop a pom-pom into the tube. What do you think will happen when you pull the balloon, then let go? Write down your predictions.

6. Pull the balloon, then let go. How far did the pom-pom travel? Use the measuring tape to record a precise answer. What do you think made it stop? Write your ideas in your science notebook.

7. Launch the pom-pom two more times from the same spot. Record how far it travels each time. Add up the three numbers, then divide by 3 to get the average distance the pom-pom traveled. Write down your observations.

MYSTERY SOLVED! Sir Isaac Newton's three Laws of Motion explain
how things move—from soccer balls to pom-poms to cars to rockets. The first law says that an object that's at rest will not start moving unless something makes it move. That's why when you put a pom-pom on the floor, it just stays there. A force has to make a resting object move. This law also says if something is moving, it won't stop moving or change direction on its own. A force is what makes a moving object change direction or stop, too.

FIREWORKS ARE SOME OF THE EARLIEST ROCKETS INVENTED!

Newton's second law says that when you apply the same force to two objects that have a different mass (how much matter is in an object), the way their motion accelerates (changes speed and/or direction) will also be different.

Newton's third law says that every time force is applied, there will be a reaction of equal force in the opposite direction. So when you pulled the balloon back you applied a force; when you let it go, the opposite reaction pushed the pom-pom forward.

TAKE 2! Want to test Newton's third law? Launch the pom-pom three more times, stretching the balloon a different amount each time—just a little, a bit more, and as far as possible. How do you think this will affect how far the pom-pom travels? Record your prediction in your science notebook, then test it out.

Free Falling

Have you ever wondered why things always fall down . . . and not up? In this experiment, we'll learn why objects seem to be attracted to the ground (and not the ceiling!), and we'll test whether there's a way we can control this force.

DIFFICULTY: MESS-O-METER: TIME: 25 MINUTES

YOU WILL NEED

Lightweight fabric, such as an old handkerchief, about 12-inch (30-cm) square

Hole punch

Small paper cup

4 12-inch (30-cm) pieces of yarn

Small, lightweight action figure or similar toy

Science notebook and pencil

→ If the hole punch is hard to use, ask an adult for help.

1. Punch a hole about ½ inch (13 mm) from each corner of the fabric with the hole punch. This is your parachute.

2. Using your hole punch, punch two holes on opposite sides of the paper cup, just under the lip. Then turn the cup a half turn and punch two more holes on opposite sides. You should now have four evenly spaced holes just under the lip of the paper cup.

3. Tie a knot at the end of each piece of yarn; the knot must be bigger than the hole you made in the paper cup. Thread one piece of yarn through each hole in the cup, so the knot is on the inside.

4. Lay the parachute out flat. Place the paper cup upside down in the center of the parachute, and line up the four holes in the cup with the holes you made in the corners of the parachute. Stretch out each piece of yarn so it makes a line from the paper cup to a corner of the parachute. Make sure none of the pieces of yarn cross each other—the yarn should make four straight lines, each running from one hole in the cup to one corner of the parachute. Thread each piece of yarn through the nearest hole in the corner of the parachute. Tie a knot on the other side of the parachute to hold the yarn in place. Now your cup is connected to the parachute.

5. It will be easier to see the results if you drop your parachute from a higher perch, such as a step stool or tall playground structure. Choose a spot to continue the experiment.

6. Drop your action figure from your high spot (without a parachute). Record your observations.

7. Retrieve your action figure. What will happen if you toss it gently upward? Write your prediction in your science notebook.

THE RECORD FOR THE MOST PARACHUTE JUMPS IN 24 HOURS IS 640!

8. Toss your action figure gently upward from the same height. Record your observations.

9. Retrieve your action figure. Now make a prediction in your science notebook: Will the small action figure fall faster or slower with the parachute?

10. Place the small action figure in the cup attached to your parachute. Hold the parachute open. then drop it from the same height. Record your observations.

MYSTERY SOLVED! Gravity is the force that pulls an object down when it drops. It causes falling objects to accelerate, or speed up, at the same rate—about 32 feet (9.75 m) per second. That means a big book and a small action figure fall at the same speed. But there's another force that acts on a falling object—resistance (it resists gravity). Resistance happens because air molecules push up against the object as gravity pulls it down. When your action figure has a parachute attached to it, the parachute captures more of this air—it resists gravity. Eventually, gravity wins. The greater the resistance, the slower the fall.

TAKE 2! Does the size of the parachute affect how slowly it falls? First, record your prediction in your science notebook. Then make a larger parachute. Keep it simple and just use empty paper cups this time. From the same height, try dropping the larger parachute alongside the smaller one and see what happens.

Puff Painting

Can you paint without a brush or even your fingers? The answer is yes—you just need a little wind to do it. Don't worry if it's not a windy day outside. You have everything you need within your own body. That's right: you have ability to create wind, and the ability to move something without touching it. It's easier than you think!

DIFFICULTY: 💪💪💪 MESS-O-METER: ✺ ✺ ✺ TIME: 15 MINUTES

YOU WILL NEED

Newspaper, enough to cover your work space

2 or 3 pieces of white 8½-by-11-inch paper

4 paper cups

Water

Measuring spoons

3 colors of washable paint

3 stirrers or spoons

Eyedropper

Paper straw

Ruler

Science notebook and pencil

Paper straw may disintegrate when wet, so have a few extras on hand in case that happens.

1. Completely cover a large work area with newspaper (or lay out newspaper on the pavement outside), then place a piece of paper on top.

2. Fill one cup with water. This will be used to clean the eyedropper. Line up the remaining three cups and put 1 teaspoon of water in each. Add 1 tablespoon of paint, a different color in each cup. Stir to combine the water and paint, using a different stirrer for each color.

3. What will happen when you gently blow on a drop of paint? Make a prediction in your science notebook.

4. Using an eyedropper, place a drop of paint on the paper. Now put the straw up to your lips and position the other end about 1 inch (2.5 cm) from the paint drop (don't let the straw touch the paint). Blow gently for 3 seconds. Observe what happens. Using the ruler, measure the distance the paint traveled and record it in your science notebook. Hint: If it seems like the paint isn't moving at all, it may be too thick. Add 1 more teaspoon of water and stir.

5. What will happen if you blow on a drop of paint more forcefully? Make a prediction in your science notebook.

6. Clean the eyedropper in the cup of water, squeezing to fill and then empty it a few times. Place a drop of a different color onto the paper. Now position the end of the straw near the drop as you did in step 4. Blow more forcefully for 3 seconds. What happens? Measure the distance the paint traveled and record it in your science notebook.

7. What will happen when you blow short, forceful bursts onto a drop of paint? Make a prediction in your science notebook.

8. Clean the eyedropper and then place a drop of the third color onto the paper. Position the end of the straw near the drop as you did in step 4. Blow three short puffs. What happens? Measure the distance the paint traveled and record it in your science notebook.

9. Compare your results. Which color of paint traveled farthest? What do you think is the reason? Let your artwork dry overnight.

MYSTERY SOLVED! Air is a mixture of gases, and moving air is called wind. When you feel the wind blow through your hair or you watch a kite sail high in the sky, you're feeling and seeing these gases at work. They move because of changes in air pressure, which is a measure of how hard air molecules press down on Earth's surface. As gravity pulls air molecules down to Earth, they push back. That force is air pressure.

When you blow on the drop of paint, you create wind, which moves the paint across the paper. The straw helps direct the force of the wind you create to a smaller area, which makes it stronger. The stronger the wind, the farther the paint travels. Muscles in your body help you breathe in and breathe out more forcefully or more gently, which is how you can create a gentle wind (as in the first example) or a strong wind (as in the second and third examples).

TAKE 2! What happens when you blow into more than one straw at the same time? What happens if you cut the straw in half? Try it out, and observe how these changes affect the distance the paint travels. With all the knowledge you've learned about how to control the paint with your breath, grab a new piece of paper and make a masterpiece!

Good Vibrations

Shh . . . do you hear that? We can't see sound waves, but they are traveling through the air around us all the time. In your science notebook, write down all the sounds you hear right now. Are they squeaky high noises or low booming sounds, or something in between? Now ask yourself: Why do those noises sound that way? In this experiment, we'll find out!

DIFFICULTY: 💪💪💪 **MESS-O-METER:** ✹ ✹ ✹ **TIME: 15 MINUTES**

YOU WILL NEED

6 glass jars (no lids) or drinking glasses, all the same size (and at least 12 ounces/360 ml)

Metal spoon

Water

Measuring cups

Liquid food coloring

Science notebook and pencil

1. Arrange the glass jars in a line. What will each jar sound like when you tap it with a spoon? Make a prediction in your science notebook. Then tap each jar. Record your observations.

2. Next, put water in each of the jars. Pour ¼ cup (60 ml) of water into the first jar. Add ½ cup (120 ml) of water to the second jar. Continue in ¼-cup increments, adding ¾ cup (180 ml) of water to the third jar, 1 cup (240 ml) of water to the fourth jar, 1¼ cups (300 ml) of water to the fifth jar, and 1½ cups (360 ml) to the sixth jar. Add a couple of drops of food coloring to each jar.

3. What will each jar sound like? Will they sound the same or different than when the container was empty? Will they sound the same or different from one another? Write your predictions in your science notebook.

4. Tap each jar with a metal spoon. Write down your observations about each jar's pitch (how high or low a sound is) in your science notebook.

MYSTERY SOLVED!

This experiment is about sound waves and pitch. Sound waves are created by vibrations, which are back-and-forth movements that are repeated again and again. Sound waves can travel through gases, like air, and they can also travel through solids, like walls, and liquids, like water.

Pitch depends on the frequency of the waves—how many are created each second. A high pitch is created by high-frequency sound waves, and can sound squeaky. A low pitch is created by low-frequency sound waves, and sounds deep and booming.

When you tapped the jar, it vibrated. The vibrations traveled from the jar to the water to the air and eventually to your ears. The jars with more water had a low pitch. The sound waves vibrated more slowly because they had more

XYLOPHONES CAN MAKE MOVIE SOUND EFFECTS LIKE CLANGING BONES.

water to travel through. The jars with less water had higher pitches. The sound waves vibrated faster because they had less water to travel through. A jar with no water in it makes the highest pitch because it has the least substance to travel through.

TAKE 2! While the xylophone you may have played in music class is made of wood and metal, you just made one out of water. Can you use the water-filled jars to play a song? Try arranging the jars in a different order to play a different tune (series of notes) when you tap the jars. You can adjust the pitch of each jar a bit by adding a little more water.

FAB FACTS ABOUT MOTION

Boom!

Lightning heats the air rapidly (to about five times hotter than the surface of the sun!) and then cools quickly. This motion creates a thunderous sound wave that can be heard for about 10 miles (16 km). You see the lightning first, then hear it. That's because light travels faster than sound.

Sounds Good

Whether you pluck a guitar string, beat a drum, or blow into a flute, different instruments make different sounds . . . but all create sound using vibration. Guitar strings vibrate when plucked or strummed. The skin of a drum vibrates when it's tapped. And air inside the tube of a flute vibrates when someone blows into it. That's music to the ears!

Supersonic

An aircraft creates shock waves in the atmosphere as it flies, just as a motorboat makes a wake in the water as it speeds along. When a jet travels faster than the speed of sound—at supersonic speed—these shock waves build up pressure that is then released. That change makes a sonic boom, a very loud noise that sounds like thunder.

Goal!

When an athlete applies spin to a ball, they alter the force of speed and change the way air flows around the ball. Spin can make a baseball curve away from a batter, direct a soccer ball around players and into the goal, or cause a ball to bounce unpredictably on a tennis court, making it hard to hit back.

Force Fields

When a skydiver jumps out of an airplane, gravity pulls them toward Earth while air resistance pushes up against them. The skydiver falls at a terminal velocity of about 10,000 feet (3,048 m) per minute. (That's the consistent speed at which an object falls once its weight is balanced by air resistance.) When the skydiver's parachute opens, it creates air resistance that alters the terminal velocity, slowing the speed of the skydiver's fall by about 90%, for a safe landing. Experiment with a parachute in **Free Falling (page 84)**.

Going Up?

The first passenger elevator, installed in 1857 in New York City, could climb 40 feet (12 m) in 1 minute. Today, the fastest elevator in China's Shanghai Tower can climb 67 feet (20 m) in 1 second. The elevator car has a streamlined shape that makes it more aerodynamic, which means there is less air resistance as it moves.

Spin-tastic

Shorter, smaller things—including people—have a lower moment of inertia. Inertia is the property whereby objects at rest stay at rest and objects in motion remain in motion unless acted on by an outside force. A lower moment of inertia means there's less resistance, resulting in faster spins. Test this at home in a wheeled chair. First, spin with your arms outstretched and note the speed of your spin. Spin again with your arms held tight to your body. Your arms created resistance, and with less resistance, you spun more quickly.

Under Pressure

What happens when a tennis ball bounces? At the factory, the ball has air pumped into it. When it hits the ground, the ball gets squished and the air inside is compressed (forced inward). The air pushes back out, and the ball returns to its original shape and shoots up off the ground. That's called elasticity.

Chapter 5

FUN AND GAMES

Whether you're dribbling a basketball, jumping over a puddle, doing a magic trick, or cutting paper for an art project, science is involved. That's because the entire world is an amazing discovery zone. Turn the pages to see how everyday activities use science, technology, engineering, art, and math concepts in different ways.

EXPERIMENTS

Strike a Pose

Balance is your body's ability to stay physically centered and supported. There are a few factors that affect your balance. Let's put one of them to the test.

DIFFICULTY: 💪💪💪   MESS-O-METER: ✴ ✴ ✴   TIME: 15 MINUTES

1. Make a chart in your science notebook like the one below.

YOU WILL NEED

Science notebook and pencil

Another person

Timer or stopwatch that can measure seconds

	EYES OPEN	EYES CLOSED
TRIAL A		
TRIAL B		
TRIAL C		
	TOTAL:	TOTAL:
	AVERAGE: (TOTAL DIVIDED BY 3)	AVERAGE: (TOTAL DIVIDED BY 3)

2. Make a prediction in your science notebook: How do you think your vision will affect your balance? Do you think you will be able to balance on one foot with your eyes open for longer, shorter, or the same amount of time as with your eyes closed?

3. Now ask a friend to time how long you can balance on one bare foot. No shoes or socks allowed! Stand on your dominant foot, which is the same as your dominant hand (the hand you write with). Bend the knee of your opposite leg like a flamingo.

4. Ask your friend to turn on the timer the second you lift up your leg, and to stop the timer the second your raised foot touches the ground. Record your time in seconds in the Trial A row and the Eyes Open column.

5. Repeat step 4 two more times and record your results in the Trial B and Trial C rows.

6. Now ask a friend to time how long you can balance on your dominant, bare foot—but this time, close your eyes just before you lift up your leg. Record your time in seconds in the Trial A row and the Eyes Closed column.

FLAMINGOS OFTEN STAND ON ONE LEG AND TUCK UP THE OTHER, WHICH SCIENTISTS BELIEVES SERVES MANY PURPOSES, FROM KEEPING THEM WARM TO HELPING THEM BALANCE WHILE THEY SLEEP.

7. Repeat step 6 two more times and record your results in the Trial B and Trial C rows.

8. Now find your averages. Add up the three numbers in the Eyes Open column, then divide by 3. Write down your average seconds in the Averages row of the Eyes Open column and circle it. Do the same for the Eyes Closed column.

9. Analyze your results. Was your prediction correct?

MYSTERY SOLVED! Your results likely showed you that you could stand on one foot for much longer with your eyes open. That's because your eyesight is key in helping your body find balance. Your eyes tell your brain how far away your body is from your surroundings, like the wall, the floor, or your friend. When you can see and your brain can interpret this data, you are more stable. But when you close your eyes, it's harder for your body to stay balanced. According to a study conducted by the National Center for Biotechnology Information, our ability to hold a one-legged pose is at its peak from our teens through our 30s. For people under the age of 40, the average balance time for standing on one foot is about 45 seconds with eyes open and around 15 seconds with eyes closed. How did your average times compare?

TAKE 2! Challenge your friend to try this activity, too. Which one of you had the better balance? Now challenge the adults in your household. Make a chart that includes the ages and balancing times of all your test subjects. Who do you think can balance longer: younger people or older people? Was your prediction correct?

zzzz...

NOT JUST YOUR EYES Luckily, your body has a few different ways to find balance. Otherwise you'd fall to the floor whenever you shut your eyes! Your inner ear is very sensitive to movement, even if you tilt your head only very slightly from left to right. Your balance also depends on the strength and flexibility of your muscles and joints. Think about the different pressures you felt on the sole of your foot as you tilted forward or on your heel as you tilted backward and tried to stay balanced. These different pressures help your body find its center point.

Paper Puzzler

Can you cut through a piece of paper and make it bigger? Write a prediction in your science notebook about what would make this possible. It's no secret—all you need is a little bit of math magic.

YOU WILL NEED

1 8½-by-11-inch piece of paper

Ruler

Pencil

Scissors

Science notebook and pencil

1. Fold a piece of paper in half lengthwise, so the fold is on the long edge. Lay it on a table lengthwise, so the folded side is to the right and the open side it to the left.

2. Using the ruler and pencil, mark the folded edge of the paper 1 inch (2.5 cm) from the bottom. (See image A.) Make nine more marks up the folded edge, each 1 inch (2.5 cm) from the other. In all, you'll have ten evenly spaced pencil marks, starting 1 inch (2.5 cm) from the bottom and top along the folded edge. You have divided the folded edge into 11 1-inch (2.5 cm) spaces.

3. On the open edge, measure 1½ inches (3.8 cm) from the bottom and mark the spot with your pencil. Make eight more marks up the open edge, each 1 inch (2.5 cm) the other. In all, you'll have nine pencil marks: a mark 1½ inches (3.8 cm) from the bottom, a mark 1½ inches (3.8 cm) from the top, and the rest 1 inch (2.5 cm) apart. (Hint: The marks on the open edge should not align with the marks on the folded edge.)

4. Use the ruler and pencil to make straight lines across the folded paper, starting at each pencil mark and extending 4 inches (10 cm). Do this from both edges of the paper, so there's a 4-inch (10-cm) line extending from each pencil mark.

5. Turn the paper sideways so the folded edge is facing you. Starting at the first pencil mark, use the scissors to cut along the 4-inch (10-cm) line toward the open edge. Don't cut all the way through—stop ¼ inch (6 mm) from the open edge. (See image B.)

6. Turn the paper around so the open edge is facing you. Starting at the first pencil mark on the open edge, cut along the 4-inch (10-cm) lines toward the folded edge. Don't cut all the way through—stop ¼ inch (6 mm) from the folded edge.

CONTINUED

MY ROOM IS 13 FEET (4 M) WIDE BY 13 FEET (4 M) LONG. ITS PERIMETER—THE LENGTH ALL THE WAY AROUND IT—IS 52 FEET (16 M).

B

D

I NEED A BIGGER PERIMETER!

7. Next, cut through the folded edge of the middle eight pieces, but not the top or bottom pieces. Find the second folded piece from the bottom and, using the scissors, carefully cut through its edge. Do this for all eight center folds, leaving the top and bottom folds intact.

8. Carefully open the paper. (See images C and D.) Look at what happened to sheet of paper. Did it change shape? Can you put your arm through it? Is it big enough to step through? (See image E.) Write down your observations in your science notebook.

MYSTERY SOLVED! By cutting the paper this way, you turned it from a sheet into a large, continuous loop. But did you actually make the paper bigger? Technically, you didn't. (In fact, there's a law in physics that says the amount of mass in an object never changes, even if it seems to get bigger or smaller.) But in the branch of math called geometry, every shape has an area and a perimeter. The area is how much space is inside the shape. The perimeter is the distance all around the outside edge. The sheet of paper is a two-dimensional rectangle. To calculate the area of any rectangle, you multiply the height by the width. An 8½-by-11-inch (21½-by-28-cm) piece of paper has an area of 93½ inches (602 cm), whole or with slits cut into it. But the perimeter of the paper did, in fact, change. And if you cut even thinner strips, the perimeter would be even bigger.

Knowing the area and perimeter of a shape is important information for architects and designers. The rooms in a building might be shaped very differently but technically be the same size. That means they would have the same area but a different perimeter. Because of this, one room might be able to have more windows or need more carpeting than another. To visualize this, imagine you are you're moving from a rectangular bedroom to a square one. The area is the same size, but the perimeter is different. That means your bed, desk, and other furniture might not fit in the new room in the same way.

TAKE 2! Have some fun with math magic. Once you've perfected this trick, perform it in front of an audience. First, challenge an audience member. Ask them to cut a hole in the paper that's big enough for them to step through. They won't be able to do it! Then grab a fresh piece of paper and wow them with your special cutting pattern. Abracadabra!

Shape-Shifter

A square is a square. A circle is a circle. There's no arguing about that! But is it possible to turn one shape into another? This is a math experiment with a big wow factor. Give it a try!

DIFFICULTY: 🌙🌙🌙　MESS-O-METER: ✴ ✴ ✴　TIME: 30 MINUTES

YOU WILL NEED

1 8½-by-11-inch piece of paper

1 8½-by-14-inch piece of paper

Scissors

Tape

Science notebook and pencil

1. From the shorter sheet of paper, cut two strips of paper 8½ inches (21.5 cm) long by 2 inches (5 cm) wide. From the longer sheet, cut two strips of paper 14 inches (35½ cm) long by 2 inches (5 cm) wide. Set the longer strips aside and work only with the shorter strips first.

2. Tape the ends of one strip together to form a loop.

3. Slip the second paper strip through the loop. Tape the two ends of the second paper strip together to form another loop. Now you have two loops that are connected. (See image A.)

4. Secure both loops to each other. To do this, place a piece of tape all the way across one loop at the spot where it meets the other one. Then do the same thing on the other loop. Test your loops to make sure they're firmly attached to each other by shaking gently.

5. Pinch one loop with your fingers to flatten it slightly, then cut a small slit through the folded edge, just big enough to fit the scissors tip. Remove your fingers, insert the tip of the scissors into the slit, and cut along the center of the loop. (See image B.) Cut all the way around—you will end up cutting through the other loop. You will have a strip with two loops, one at each end. (See image C.)

6. Starting at the loop at one end, cut through the center of the wide, straight strip. (See image D.) Continue cutting it from end to end, from one loop through the other. Gently pull apart the two sides of the strip you just cut. (See image E.) What shape are you left with? Write your observations in your science notebook.

7. Now follow steps 2 through 6 with the longer strips. What do you think will happen with longer pieces? Write your predictions in your science notebook.

8. Assemble, tape, and cut the longer strips of paper in the same way you did with the shorter strips. Do the results match your prediction? Write down your observations.

MYSTERY SOLVED!

In geometry, there are rules (proven facts) about the shapes we see in our world. These tell us that shapes consistently perform in specific ways. Engineers and architects use these rules to construct buildings, rocket scientists use them to design spacecraft, and urban planners use them to help cities grow. You also used them for this experiment to show that, thanks to the rules of geometry, the results will be the same every time. It doesn't matter what size your loops are—if you attach them this way and cut them this way, they will always turn into a square. The only difference is the size, not shape—longer strips mean a larger square. This is how you used rules of geometry to turn two circles into a square!

DATING BACK 5,000 YEARS, PAPYRUS WAS USED BY THE ANCIENT EGYPTIANS FOR MANY PURPOSES, NOTABLY FOR WRITING PAPER.

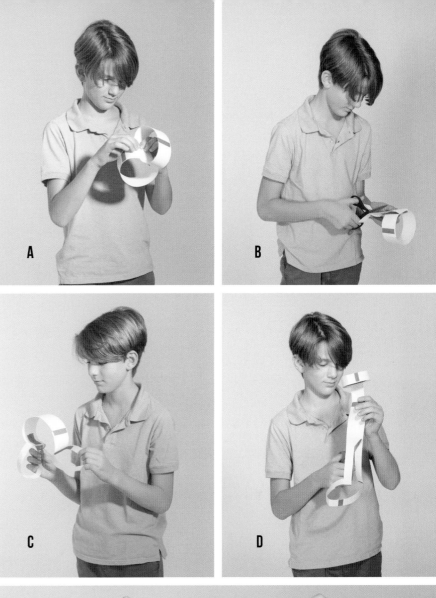

A

B

C

D

E

Attract and Repel

Take a look at your refrigerator. Are there magnets holding up some artwork, papers, or coupons? If not, there probably are magnets in the fridge and freezer—in many models they hold the doors tightly closed. How do magnets work, and why do they stick to a refrigerator but not to the wall? In this experiment, we'll look at how magnets work and why some things are magnetic and others aren't.

DIFFICULTY: 💪💪💪   MESS-O-METER: ✺ ✺ ✺   TIME: 20 MINUTES

YOU WILL NEED

Magnet

Large steel paper clip (not plastic-coated)

2 paper plates

Crayons or markers

Scissors

Science notebook and pencil

1. Pick up your magnet in one hand and your paper clip in the other. Bring the two items close together. What happens? Write your observations in your science notebook.

2. Now pick up the magnet and a paper plate. Bring the magnet close to the paper plate. What happens? Write down your observations.

3. To figure out how and why magnets work, let's go on an animal safari. On one of the plates, use the crayons or markers to draw four of your favorite animals. Leave about 2 inches (5 cm) between each animal.

4. Using a marker, draw a continuous line on the paper plate that travels near all the animals. This will be your road. Write START at one edge of the line and END at the other.

5. Draw a car on the second plate. It should be about 2 inches (5 cm) long and 1 inch (2.5 cm) wide. Cut out the car and slide it into the paper clip. This will be your vehicle for the animal safari.

6. Now place the paper clip car at START on the plate where you drew the road. Hold up the plate with one hand, and with the other, hold the magnet beneath the plate, just under the paper clip car. Move the magnet back and forth just a little. What happens?

7. Move your paper clip car along the road toward END, visiting the animals along the safari route. Does it matter if the magnet is touching the bottom of the plate, or can it be a slight distance away? Write down your observations about how magnets work.

THE DARK STRIP ON THE BACK OF A GIFT CARD, CREDIT CARD, OR HOTEL KEY CARD IS CALLED A MAGSTRIPE. IT CONTAINS MICROSCOPIC MAGNETIC PARTICLES.

MYSTERY SOLVED! Magnets are surrounded by an invisible force called a magnetic field. This magnetic field attracts (pulls toward it) anything that is magnetic. Certain metals, including steel paper clips, become temporarily magnetized, or attracted to magnets. Paper does not. You saw this when you held the paper clip next to the magnet in step 1 and then next to the paper plate in step 2. When you move the magnet underneath the plate, the paper clip moves because it is attracted to the magnet, and the magnetic field is strong enough to pass through the paper to the paper clip.

TAKE 2! Will your experiment work with different types of paper? What do you think will happen if you stack up two paper plates, or three? Will it work through cardboard? Write down your predictions, then try these different materials to see what happens.

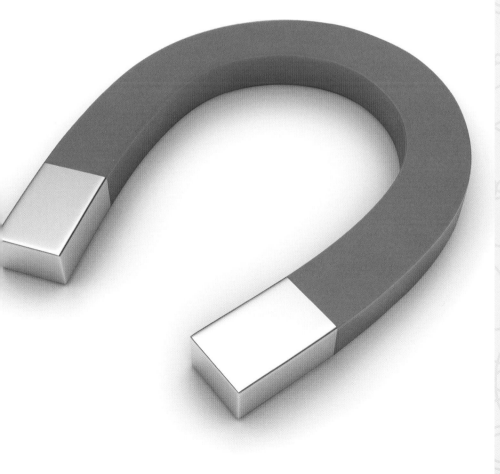

GH KITCHEN APPLIANCES LAB

OUR EXPERT SAYS

"Magnets sometimes hide in plain sight. Inside most microwaves, there's a unit called a magnetron that usually contains a pair of magnets. It creates the microwaves that make the water molecules in food vibrate. This vibration creates heat and cooks your food much faster than a traditional oven can—sometimes in just a minute or two!"

—Nicole Papantoniou
Deputy Director, Kitchen Appliances & Technology Lab

Let's Bounce

All balls are round. Most, like basketballs and soccer balls, are shaped like a sphere. Some—like American footballs—are ovals. Some have holes (Whiffle balls), some have dimples (golf balls), and some are fuzzy (tennis balls). What makes balls bounce? And do they always bounce the same way? Where does their energy come from? Write down your best educated guesses in your science notebook, then let's explore the physics of bouncing balls.

DIFFICULTY: 💪💪💪   MESS-O-METER: ✸ ✸ ✸   TIME: 20 MINUTES

1. Make a chart with three columns, like the one below. Label them as shown.

TRIAL A	TRIAL B	TRIAL C

2. Next, make a prediction in your science notebook: When a ball strikes a hard surface, will it always bounce back up to the same height? What affects how high a ball will bounce?

3. Find a safe place outdoors where you can bounce balls on a hard surface, like a driveway or basketball court or playground at the park. Or use an indoor space with an uncarpeted floor, like the garage, a workshop, or a basement (if bouncing balls indoors is okay with a parent or other adult).

4. With the tennis ball in your hand, straighten your arm directly in front of your body at shoulder height and simply let the ball drop from your hand. Did the ball reach knee height, waist height, shoulder height, or head height when it bounced back up? Record your result in the row under Trial A in your science notebook.

5. Now, with the tennis ball in your hand, bend your elbow and tuck your arm next to your body so the ball is at shoulder height. Throw the ball down without untucking your arm. Did the ball reach knee height, waist height, shoulder height, or head height when it bounced back up? Record your result in the row under Trial B.

SERENA WILLIAMS'S FASTEST SERVE ROCKETED IN AT NEARLY 129 MILES PER HOUR (207 KPH).

6. Holding the ball over your head, throw it down to the ground more forcefully. How high did it bounce? Write that down in the row under Trial C. Now compare your results. Was your prediction correct?

MYSTERY SOLVED!
When you lifted the tennis ball up to your shoulder, you used some energy to do that. That energy was transferred to the ball as stored, or potential, energy. When the ball moves (drops), its potential energy becomes kinetic energy (the energy of movement). Then, when the ball hits the ground, some of the energy is absorbed by the floor, some is turned into sound waves (the sound the ball makes when it hits the floor), and some is even turned into heat. When the tennis ball was dropped, it didn't bounce as high as the height from which it was dropped, because some of that energy changed into heat, which could not be reused.

The more forcefully you threw the tennis ball to the ground, the higher it bounced. The force you used gave the ball more energy. When a ball has more energy on its way down, it will also have more energy on its way up.

TAKE 2!
Try this experiment on a soft surface, like grass. First, make a prediction: Will the hardness of a surface affect the bounce height? Why? Then check it out. Was your prediction correct?

GH ENGINEERING & TECH LAB

OUR EXPERT SAYS

"Tennis balls have more air pressure inside them than there is in the air around them, which helps them bounce (more air pressure equals a higher bounce). When used in a game, they begin to leak air, and with every hit or bounce, they lose some of their internal air pressure. Lower air pressure means a lower bounce, and that's why professional tennis players replace their balls frequently during play."

—Rachel Rothman
Chief Technologist & Director of Engineering

Boing Boing

Most people have a preferred hand—they do everyday tasks with either the left or right hand. Whichever hand you write with, that's your dominant hand. Does that also mean that your dominant hand (and arm) is better at sports than the other? If so, can a little practice make a difference? Make a prediction in your science notebook.

DIFFICULTY: MESS-O-METER: TIME: 10 MINUTES

YOU WILL NEED

Science notebook and pencil

Tennis racket (or table tennis paddle)

Tennis ball (or table tennis ball)

1. Make a chart in your science notebook with four columns and three rows, like the one below. Label them as shown.

	TRIAL 1	TRIAL 2	TRIAL 3
LEFT ARM			
RIGHT ARM			

2. Hold the tennis racket in your left hand and the tennis ball in your right hand. Hold the racket horizontally in front of your body at about waist level, with your elbow bent. The racket strings should be facing up, parallel to the ground. Drop the ball gently onto the center of the racket and begin bouncing the ball upward gently. How many times can you bounce the ball before it drops to the floor? Record your result in the Trial 1 column next to Left Arm.

3. Repeat step 2 two more times and record your results in the columns Trial 2 and Trial 3 in the Left Arm row.

4. Hold the tennis racket in your right hand and the tennis ball in your left hand. Hold the racket horizontally in front of your body at about waist level, with your elbow bent. The racket strings should be facing up, parallel to the ground. Drop the ball gently onto the center of the racket and begin bouncing the ball upward gently. How many times can you bounce the ball before it drops to the floor? Record your result in the Trial 1 column next to Right Arm.

CATS ARE MORE THAN THREE TIMES AS LIKELY TO BE LEFT-HANDED AS PEOPLE ARE.

5. Repeat step 4 two more times and record your results in the columns Trial 2 and Trial 3 in the Right Arm row.

6. Review your results. Which arm was able to bounce the ball more times in each trial? Did it change from trial to trial? Was your prediction correct?

MYSTERY SOLVED! Did you predict that your dominant arm would be able to bounce the ball more times in a row than your nondominant arm? That's true for most people. Studies estimate that 85% to 90% of people are right-handed. The rest are left-handed, except for about 1% of people who are ambidextrous (can use both hands equally well). Scientists are still trying to better understand why humans have different hand dominance. One hypothesis is that a gene passed down from parents to child may be tied to left- or right-handedness, which would mean people are born with a preference. Another possibility is that hand dominance is a combination between genes and environment. Babies enter a world of mainly right-handed people and products engineered for right-handed people. And that may contribute to why so many people are right-handed.

TAKE 2! You can improve the ability of your nondominant arm with practice. Give your nondominant arm a few more practice rounds every day over the next week. Then try the experiment again. Were you able to bounce the ball more times after practicing?

MEOW! I'M NOT LEFT-HANDED, I'M LEFT-PAWED.

Go for It!

A volleyball player spiking a ball, a goalie leaping to block a high shot, and a basketball player going for a slam dunk all have something in common: they're jumping. And they're not just any jumps—they have power and distance. But what is a jump, really? Your knees bend and your feet push off the floor. Are those the only parts of your body that make a difference when jumping? Make a prediction in your science notebook and let's find out!

DIFFICULTY: 💪💪💪 **MESS-O-METER:** ✳✳✳ **TIME: 20 MINUTES**

YOU WILL NEED

Science notebook and pencil

Painter's tape or other nonstick tape

Scissors

Tape measure

1. In your science notebook, make a chart with two columns and four rows, like the one below. Label the rows as shown.

TRIAL A: ARMS DOWN	
TRIAL B: ARMS DOWN, DEEP KNEE BEND	
TRIAL C: ARMS SWINGING	
TRIAL D: ARMS SWINGING, DEEP KNEE BEND	

2. Make a prediction in your science notebook: Which arm position will enable you to jump the farthest?

3. Cut a strip of tape 2 feet (61 cm) long and stick it on the floor. This is your starting line. Cut a second, short piece of tape. Stick it to your shirt.

4. Hold your arms against your sides, hands facing the floor. With your knees slightly bent, jump forward. Before you move, remove the tape from your shirt and place it on the floor just behind your heel.

5. Then, get the tape measure and calculate the distance from the starting line to your first jump. Record it in the box for Trial A in your science notebook.

6. For Trial B, cut another short piece of tape, then repeat steps 4 and 5, this time starting with a deeper knee bend. Record the result.

THE LONGEST LONG JUMP ON RECORD IS 8.95 METERS (29.36 FT).

THAT'S AS LONG AS A MEDIUM-SIZE SCHOOL BUS.

7. For Trial C, cut another short piece of tape, then repeat steps 4 and 5, but this time use your arms. As you bend your knees, swing your arms back. Then, when you push off to jump, swing your arms forward. Record your result.

8. For Trial D, cut another short piece of tape, then use your arms again, but this time bend your knees as deeply as you did in Trial B. Record the distance of your jump on the chart.

9. Review your chart. In which trial did you jump the farthest? Was it all about the legs and knees, or did the arms make a difference? And did it matter how deeply you bent your knees? Do the results match your prediction?

MYSTERY SOLVED! The stronger and faster you are, the higher and farther you can jump. When you bend your knees and get ready to jump, the muscles in your body contract, creating a force that pushes into the ground. As you jump, the stored-up potential energy in your muscles and legs releases like a rubber band snapping. The deeper you bend your knees, the more potential energy you store and the longer you jump. Boing!

As you discovered, your arms matter, too—where they are and how you use them. Most likely, your shortest jump was when your arms were at your sides, and your longest jump was when you swung your arms forward. The arm movement created even more force, which pushed your body into the ground even more. More downward force meant more upward force, so you could jump farther.

TAKE 2! Challenge friends or family members to a jump-off. Who do you think will have the longest leap? Why? Is it all about the knee bend and arm swings, or will it matter how tall a person is or how long their legs and arms are? Hint: Each person's body is different, so people the exact same size may have different results. Make a prediction, then compare the results with what you expected to happen.

Act Fast!

Someone tosses you a flying disc. It's getting closer and closer. You start running toward it, arms extended, ready for the catch, but—*whoosh*—it flies right past your fingertips. You've just missed it! Sometimes your body can't react quite as fast as you think it can. This two-person experiment tests reaction times—how quickly your body responds to something it senses.

DIFFICULTY: 💪💪💪   MESS-O-METER: ✦ ✦ ✦   TIME: 10 MINUTES

YOU WILL NEED

Science notebook and pencil

12-inch (30-cm) wood ruler

Another person

1. Make a chart with two columns and five rows in your science notebook, like the one below. Label them as shown.

TRIAL A	
TRIAL B	
TRIAL C	
	TOTAL:
	AVERAGE: (TOTAL DIVIDED BY 3)

2. Stand with your dominant arm (the hand you write with) at your side and bend the elbow up and out. Your arm will form the shape of an L. Hold your thumb and index finger apart like a claw—you're getting ready to catch a falling ruler.

3. Ask your friend to grip the ruler at the 12-inch (30-cm) mark and hold it vertically just above your outstretched hand.

4. Without giving you a warning, your friend should let go of the ruler, dropping it between your thumb and forefinger. Your goal is to catch it as quickly as you can between your thumb and index finger. Don't move your fingers before the ruler falls.

5. When you catch the ruler, hold on to it. Note the place on the ruler where your fingers caught the ruler and record the measurement in your science notebook. It could be at the 2-inch (5-cm) mark or at the 9-in (23-cm) mark. Or it might have slipped through your fingers altogether.

A DOCTOR TAPS YOUR KNEE WITH A RUBBER MALLET TO TEST YOUR REFLEXES.

DOCTORS TEST REFLEXES IN OTHER PLACES, LIKE ANKLES AND ELBOWS, TOO.

6. Repeat steps 2 through 5 twice more and record the results. Did your reaction time change? Write down your observations.

7. Add up the results from each trial. Divide that number by 3. This is your average of the three inch or centimeter marks where you caught the ruler. Rounding up or down to the nearest inch, look for your average on the chart below. If your average result was 8 inches (20 cm), your reaction time was 0.20 seconds, or one-fifth of a second.

If you caught the ruler at:	Reaction time is:
2 inch (5 cm)	0.10 seconds
4 inches (10 cm)	0.14 seconds
6 inches (15 cm)	0.17 seconds
8 inches (20 cm)	0.20 seconds
10 inches (25 cm)	0.23 seconds
12 inches (30 cm)	0.25 seconds

MYSTERY SOLVED! The reaction time shows how long it took for your brain to send a message to your body. First, your eyes saw the ruler dropping and sent a message to your the visual cortex (the part of the brain that's responsible for understanding what you see). Then it sent a message to the motor cortex (the part of the brain that's responsible for moving your muscles). The motor cortex sent a message down your spinal cord (which runs from the base of your brain down the center of your back), into your arm, and finally to your hand, telling your finger muscles to move. The farther the ruler fell before you caught it, the slower your reaction time was.

TAKE 2! Repeat the experiment again with your nondominant hand. But first, make a prediction: Do you think the reaction times will be the same? If not, why not? Can you improve your reaction time with repeated attempts?

FAB FACTS ABOUT PLAY

Pump It Up

How do skateboarders convert energy more efficiently, move faster, and go higher? They crouch down and then straighten up. That action of bending the knees and then pushing up is called pumping. When you bend your knees, you increase your potential energy. When you push up, you convert that to kinetic energy (the energy of motion).

Whee!

Roller coasters don't need electricity to work—they rely on other scientific forces. Coaster cars collect potential energy as they climb up a steep incline. When they crest the top of the hill, gravity takes over and potential energy becomes kinetic energy as the cars speed down the tracks. The shape of the tracks works with or against gravity, directing cars down or up hills. This cycle continues until the cars reach the flat track and coast to the finish line.

Hoop It Up

When you swivel your hips with a Hula-Hoop around your waist, you create a twisting force, called torque. This spins the hoop around. You also create an upward force that keeps the hoop above your hips. Friction between your clothing and the hoop slows down the hoop—but it also helps it stay on your waist.

Let the Games Begin

Scientists have found that playing video games can actually change your brain. Some video game players get better at focusing their attention more quickly and paying attention longer. Scientists also discovered that the area of the brain that is in charge of identifying objects visually and understanding the differences and similarities between objects gets larger.

Superb Snow Fort

What does a snow fort have in common with a sandcastle? Both need water. Dry snow is too loose and powdery to stick together. Slushy wet snow has too much water to hold a shape. But damp snow is just right. The water molecules bond like glue, making it easier for snow to hold a shape.

Sand Castle Secret

It's called a sandcastle, but water is the key to a successful construction. Dry sand can't hold a shape. The water in damp sand coats each grain. When individual water molecules stick together, they form a strong bond. Each water-coated grain of sand sticks to other water-coated grains of sand and thus, your masterpiece.

Flop or Dive?

Water molecules at the top of a body of water are strongly bonded together because of surface tension, forming a barrier that resists any external force. When you belly flop into a pool, your body pushes down and the surface tension of the water pushes up. Ouch! But when you dive in, you hit the water only with your fingertips. Less surface area on your fingers means less resistance from the surface of the water, allowing the rest of your body to slide in painlessly.

POWER WORKOUTS

What does it take to excel at sports? Athletes spend a lot of time training, and a lot of their focus is on strength, size, and speed. What role does science play?

Skill Drills

A study that analyzed the University of Queensland (Australia) soccer team found that while being big, strong, and fast matters, the most successful athletes were those with the best skills. A skill is something you learn, practice, and get better at, such as the ability to pass the ball with great control and accuracy. Whether or not you're the biggest, fastest, or strongest, you can become better at your sport by working hard to improve your skills.

Agility Tests

Agility is the ability to quickly change the direction or speed of your body when you are moving. Think of a football receiver with the ball who runs left, then quickly dodges right to avoid being tackled on the way to scoring a touchdown. You change course, stay in control, and keep your momentum all at the same time. That's not easy! Dogs do this, too, in competitions called agility trials.

To work on your agility skills, take a tip from the pros. In a yard or park, place five cones (or tennis balls or other markers) about 10 feet (3 m) apart in a zigzag pattern, which you will run around. The pattern should ensure that you have to change your body's direction each time you pass a cone or marker. Then ask a friend to time you. Run the course as fast as you can, rounding the markers on alternating sides. Try practicing a few times a week to see if you can improve your time with more practice.

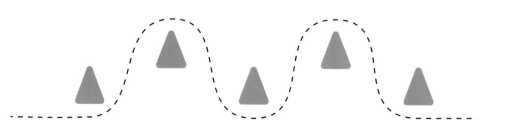

Putting It All Together

The top basketball stars have record-setting accomplishments. What makes them stand out from all the rest?

The average NBA player is 6 feet 6.5 inches (199 cm) tall and can jump up more than 2 feet (61 cm). Basketball star LeBron James is just 2 inches (5 cm) taller than average, but he can jump more than 3 feet (91 cm) high. How can such a small increase in body height result in about a 50% improvement in jumping height? Additional forces like strength, speed, and skills work together to account for the difference. LeBron is considered one of the best at "seeing" the game—observing and understanding what's going on all around. This helps him anticipate what's going to happen and be ahead of others in actions and reactions.

Steph Curry is the master of the 3-point shot. He's not the tallest player on the court, but he's fast and agile. Balance and coordination also give him an edge when he's shooting the ball. He positions his feet for balance, and his ankles, knees, and hips pump at the same time when he jumps. Another skill is focus: in the way he practices and by clearing his mind before taking a shot, Curry uses his mental as well as physical powers. Every athlete has unique advantages—look for yours as you work on your skills.

Making the Grade

What makes an athlete the best in his or her sport? Can you make a guess by following some scientific principles?

Write down a list ranking your favorite five or ten athletes. Then think about all the different aspects of being good at sports. There's strength and speed, for sure. Size is relative—being smaller is more of an advantage for a gymnast than a basketball player. Do any of your favorites have special moves that make them stand out? And how important is resilience—the ability to recover quickly from a disappointment or loss? And then there's teamwork to consider. Now look at your list again. Based on your analysis, would you change the ranking of your faves?

Invisible Invaders

Sometimes you can see that it's time to wash your hands. But even when your hands *look* clean, they may be covered with germs you can't see. Soap is your partner in grime: it grabs the germs that then wash away when you rinse!

Chapter 6

SLIME AND GRIME

Here's a not-so-secret fact: slime and grime can be gross but also super fun! In this chapter, chemistry will lead the way as you explore how to spot and interact with bacteria, mold, fungus, and more. But be warned: things might get a little stinky, gooey, or downright yucky!

EXPERIMENTS

Slime Time

In this experiment, you'll combine a few simple ingredients to make a soft and stretchy substance that's super satisfying to pull and squish.

DIFFICULTY: 💪💪💪   MESS-O-METER: ✸ ✸ ✸   TIME: 15 MINUTES

YOU WILL NEED

Science notebook and pencil

Bowl

1 cup (240 ml) white glue

Liquid food coloring

1 teaspoon baking soda

1 tablespoon contact lens saline solution (must list boric acid and sodium borate in ingredients)

Towel for drying your hands

SAFETY TIP

Borax can be irritating when exposed to skin. Avoid contact with eyes and do not drink or eat.

THERE'S SLIME IN YOUR NOSE—IT'S CALLED MUCUS!

1. In your science notebook, list your ingredients (glue, food coloring, baking soda, saline solution), and leave space to write down observations for each one.

2. Before mixing the ingredients together, analyze them. How would you describe each stand-alone ingredient: is it a solid, a liquid, or something in between? Record your observations in your science notebook.

3. Pour the glue in the bowl. Start by adding 3 to 5 drops of food coloring, then stir. What does the color look like? Now add more—up to 10 drops to create a deeper color—stirring well to combine.

4. Add baking soda and stir. Then add saline solution. Stir until the mixture thickens and is too firm to stir.

5. Knead the slime in the bowl. Use the heel of your hand to push the slime down and away. Give the slime a quarter turn, fold over, and press down again. Continue kneading until it solidifies. Observe the changes that happen as you knead.

6. Now play with your slime: pull it, push it, and stretch it! Is it a solid, liquid, or something in between? Wash and dry your hands, then record your observations in your science notebook.

7. Store your slime in a sealed container. It will last for up to two weeks, depending on how often you play with it.

NOTE IT! Don't get slime in your hair—it'll stick. If you do, ask an adult to help you by massaging a little vegetable oil into your hair, and then gently combing out the slime.

TAKE 2! What happens if you make this slime recipe but add more saline solution? How does it affect how the slime behaves? What if you add water? How do the two versions compare?

Oo-Oo-Oobleck

In this slime-tastic experiment, you will explore different states of matter. As you learned in Core Concepts on page 12, the state of matter—liquid, solid, or gas—can be altered by changing its temperature. But are there other ways to change the state of a liquid? Make some oobleck—a name inspired by a book by Dr. Seuss—to see what happens and why.

DIFFICULTY: 💪💪💪 **MESS-O-METER:** ✳ ✳ ✳ **TIME: 15 MINUTES**

YOU WILL NEED

Bowl

1½ cups (192 g) cornstarch

1 cup (240 ml) water

Mixing spoon or spatula

5 drops green liquid food coloring

Science notebook and pencil

Towel for drying your hands

1. In a bowl, add the cornstarch and water and stir with a mixing spoon or spatula. The mixture will be gooey. Add the food coloring and stir to combine.

2. Now write down an observation in your science notebook: How would you describe this mixture? Does it look like a liquid or a solid?

3. Dip your fingers into the bowl. Press hard. What happens? Wash and dry your hands, then write down your observations.

4. Slightly tip the bowl from left to right, being careful not to spill the mixture. Does the mixture move back and forth in the bowl? Record your observations.

5. Pick up a small amount of the mix and squeeze it. What happens? Wash and dry your hands, then record your observations in your science notebook.

6. Store your oobleck in a covered container for up to a couple of days. It will dry out over time or when left out.

TAKE 2! Play around with the balance of cornstarch and water by adding more water. Try using something different, like a whisk, to stir it up. What happens? Now add more cornstarch. What happens? Record your observations.

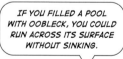

IF YOU FILLED A POOL WITH OOBLECK, YOU COULD RUN ACROSS ITS SURFACE WITHOUT SINKING.

MYSTERY SOLVED! Sir Isaac Newton, a mathematician and scientist who lived more than 300 years ago, discovered that most fluids have a constant or unchanging viscosity (the ease with which they flow). Water, saline solution, and glue are examples of Newtonian fluids with constant viscosities. Water and saline solution have a low viscosity, which means they always flow easily and quickly because there's less friction. Glue has a high viscosity and therefore always flows more slowly.

When the ingredients in each of these experiments are combined with a solid (either baking soda or cornstarch), they may look like a liquid at first. But as you apply more pressure (by pushing, pulling, touching, or squeezing), it causes them to act differently. Their viscosity changes. So much so that they don't act like a liquid or a solid!

Sometimes slime's viscosity is low (wet, sticky, and stretchy) and sometimes it's high (more firm and rubbery, like Silly Putty or chewing gum). It behaves differently with less or more stress (pressure). With less stress, it feels stickier and more like a liquid; with more stress, it sticks to itself, like a solid would. Oobleck looks like a liquid, but when you push or squeeze it, it feels like a solid. The pressure you've added moves the water (liquid) out of the way, so you're mostly feeling the cornstarch (which is a solid). So what does that make slime and oobleck? They are both non-Newtonian fluids, also known as soft solids. Ketchup is another non-Newtonian fluid. So are toothpaste, shampoo, and honey. Even boogers (mucus) are considered a non-Newtonian fluid. Yuck!

SAFETY TIP Don't pour these mixtures down the drain. They will clog pipes, and now you know why! Instead, dump your slime and oobleck into the garbage or a compost bin.

Grime Fighters

Most silver-colored coins—like nickels, dimes, and quarters—look fairly bright and shiny. But copper-coated coins, like pennies, almost always look dull, covered by brown, black, or even green markings. Is it dirt or something else that darkens them? In this experiment, you'll test a few ways to clean pennies and find out exactly what causes them to change color.

DIFFICULTY: 💪💪💪 MESS-O-METER: ✦ ✦ ✦ TIME: 45 MINUTES

YOU WILL NEED

5 sticky notes

Pencil

5 small glasses or plastic cups

¼ cup (60 ml) white vinegar

¼ cup (60 ml) lemon juice

¼ cup (60 ml) dish soap

¼ cup (60 ml) ketchup

¼ cup (60 ml) milk

2 teaspoons salt

Spoon

15 dull pennies or other copper coins

Timer or stopwatch

Science notebook

1. On your sticky notes, write: Vinegar, Lemon Juice, Dish Soap, Ketchup, and Milk. Place them in a row on a counter or table.

2. Set out each of the five cups in front of a labeled sticky note. Pour each liquid into the cup with that liquid's name on the sticky note. For example, pour ¼ cup (60 ml) vinegar in a cup and place it in front of the vinegar label. Do the same with each other liquid.

3. Add 1 teaspoon salt to the vinegar and stir with a spoon to dissolve. Rinse and dry the spoon. Add 1 teaspoon salt to the lemon juice and stir with a spoon to dissolve.

4. Place three pennies in each cup. Make a prediction in your science notebook: Which solution will clean a penny best? Set your timer for 10 minutes.

5. When the timer goes off, remove one penny from the Vinegar cup. Rinse, dry, and place it on the left-hand edge of the sticky note in front of the cup it was soaking in. Do the same with a penny from each of the other cups. Observe the pennies—do they look different from one another?

6. Set the timer for another 10 minutes. When the timer goes off, remove a second penny from each cup. Rinse, dry, and place in the middle of the sticky note, next to the 10-minute penny. Compare the 10-minute penny to the 20-minute penny. Write down your observations.

7. Set the timer for another 10 minutes, then remove the final penny from each cup. Rinse, dry, and place the third penny to the right of the sticky note, next to the 20-minute penny. Compare the 20-minute penny to the 30-minute penny. Write down your observations.

8. Study all of the pennies. Does one look shinier than the others? Do any still look dull? Make an educated guess in your science notebook as to why certain liquids worked the way they did.

MYSTERY SOLVED! Pennies are coated with copper. Oxygen molecules in the air bond (join) with copper molecules to form copper oxide—that brown and black tarnish you see on the penny. So the pennies aren't dirty—they're oxidized.

A solution that is acidic (like vinegar or lemon juice) can slowly dissolve the copper oxide buildup. Salt is a catalyst—something that speeds up the rate of a chemical reaction without altering it—making the vinegar and lemon juice act more quickly. The longer the pennies sit in the solution, the more copper oxide is removed and the brighter they will be. The pennies soaked in the vinegar-and-salt and lemon-and-salt solutions should look brighter and shinier than before. The pennies soaked in the ketchup should look brighter, too. That's because ketchup contains tomatoes, which are acidic, and salt. Milk and dish soap are not acidic and do not contain salt, so they cannot dissolve copper oxides.

TAKE 2! Place all five pennies in the vinegar-and-salt solution for 15 minutes, but this time don't rinse them after you remove them from the cup. Let them sit overnight on a paper plate. Check them the next day. What has happened?

What Mold Told Us

The surfaces you touch every day—and even your own hands—are super germy. Even if they look clean, they're covered in microorganisms that are too small to see. Try this experiment to see which everyday objects host the most germs.

DIFFICULTY: 💪💪💪　MESS-O-METER: ✹ ✹ ✹　45 MINUTES HANDS-ON; 3 WEEKS TOTAL

YOU WILL NEED

6 sticky notes

Pencil

6 resealable plastic bags

Gloves or kitchen tongs

6 slices of bakery-style white bread

Paper or clean plate

Wet kitchen sponge or dishrag

Doorknob

Cellphone, tablet, keyboard, or remote control

Toilet seat

Unwashed hands

Science notebook and pencil

→ Wear gloves or use tongs to remove bread slices from the package and place them on the plate without touching them.

1. On your sticky notes, write: Untouched, Kitchen, Doorknob, Technology, Toilet, and Dirty Hands. Add the date to each sticky note, then affix one to each of the plastic bags.

2. Using gloves or kitchen tongs, pick up a slice of bread without touching it and place it in the bag labeled Untouched. Seal the bag tightly.

3. Using gloves or kitchen tongs, pick up another slice of bread without touching it and wipe it across the kitchen sponge or dishrag. Place the bread in the bag labeled Kitchen. Seal the bag tightly.

4. Using gloves or kitchen tongs, pick up another slice of bread without touching it and wipe it across your bedroom doorknob. Place the bread in the bag labeled Doorknob and seal the bag tightly.

5. Using gloves or kitchen tongs, pick up another slice of bread without touching it and wipe it across the front and back of a piece of technology, like a remote control, cellphone, tablet, or keyboard. Place the bread in the bag labeled Technology and seal the bag tightly.

6. Using gloves or kitchen tongs, pick up another slice of bread without touching it and wipe it across the toilet seat. Place the bread in the bag labeled Toilet and seal the bag tightly.

7. Wipe the last slice of bread across both of your unwashed palms. Place it in the bag labeled Dirty Hands and seal it tightly. Place all six bags on a counter or shelf or in a dark drawer or closet where they can be undisturbed for three weeks.

8. Wash your hands with soap and water for at least 20 seconds. Then, in your science notebook, make a prediction: Which slices of bread will grow the least mold? The most? Why? Rank them from 1 (least mold) to 6 (most mold).

CONTINUED

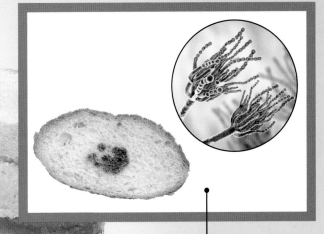

Mold spores (shown here) need nutrients, moisture, and the right temperature to grow.

9. Now comes the hard part—waiting! Observe your bags after 7 days, 14 days, and then 21 days. Make a chart like the one below in your science notebook, and record your observations. After 21 days, throw the sealed bags away.

	7 DAYS	14 DAYS	21 DAYS
UNTOUCHED			
KITCHEN			
DOOR			
TECHNOLOGY			
BATHROOM			
DIRTY HANDS			

BREAD GOES STALE MUCH FASTER IN THE REFRIGERATOR THAN ON THE KITCHEN COUNTER.

THE DIRTY DETAILS Research shows that cell phones are dirtier than toilets. Did this hold true in your experiment? Phones and sinks often have more germs than toilets do, because you touch those surfaces so frequently. One study found fecal matter (poop particles) on 60% of cell phones tested. That's a good reminder to wash your hands frequently—after using the toilet every time and throughout the day!

MYSTERY SOLVED! You will notice that the bag labeled Untouched has very little mold, while the others have a lot of mold. How did that mold get there?

Mold is a fungus that appears when microorganisms like bacteria find an environment they like and start to reproduce. In this experiment, bacteria from various surfaces around your home were transferred to the bread. They fed off the bread and continued to grow and reproduce. These growths are called colonies. They could be green, yellow, white, gray, or black, and can sometimes also be fuzzy.

Now the question is: How did the bacteria get on those surfaces? From you and from anyone else who touched them! Observe the slice of bread that was wiped across your unwashed palms. Yuck, right? And everyone in your home probably touches the remote, so that's even more germs. Humans touch a lot of surfaces during the day, which spreads bacteria from hands to surfaces over and over again. That's why frequent handwashing is so important.

NOTE IT! Mold will grow on all types of bread. The more preservatives bread has, the longer it will take for mold to grow. Using fresh bakery-style bread will help your experiment progress more quickly.

TAKE 2! What do you think will get your hands cleanest: water, soap and water, hand sanitizer, or disinfecting wipes? Make a prediction, then repeat the experiment by touching bread with dirty hands, water-cleaned hands, soap-and-water-cleaned hands, and so on. Which gives you the cleanest hands?

SAFETY TIP Keep the bags sealed throughout the experiment. Some people are allergic to mold, and it can be dangerous to breathe in. Do not open the bags at any time and don't eat the bread.

Don't Forget to Brush

You brush your teeth at least twice a day, but why? Minty toothpaste makes your breath smell fresh, but what else does toothpaste do? To show how it protects your teeth, try this egg-cellent experiment.

DIFFICULTY: 💪💪💪 MESS-O-METER: ✸ ✸ ✸ TIME: 15 MINUTES HANDS-ON; 12 HOURS TOTAL

YOU WILL NEED

4 sticky notes

Pencil

4 glasses or plastic containers large enough to hold an egg

Brown soda (like cola or root beer)

Lemon juice

4 hard-boiled white eggs, at room temperature

Small bowl

1 tube toothpaste with fluoride

Towel

Science notebook and pencil

To bring eggs to room temperature, let them sit out on a counter for about 1 hour before beginning the experiment.

1. Write on the sticky notes: Soda 1, Soda 2, Juice 1, and Juice 2. Place them in a row on a counter.

2. Fill two glasses halfway with brown soda and place behind the Soda 1 and Soda 2 sticky notes. Fill two glasses halfway with lemon juice and place behind the Juice 1 and Juice 2 sticky notes.

3. Carefully place one egg in the bowl. Squeeze a big dollop—about one tablespoon—of toothpaste on top of the egg and gently rub the toothpaste all around with your hands until the egg is completely covered in a thick layer of toothpaste. Repeat with a second egg.

4. Gently submerge the toothpaste-covered eggs into the liquids: one egg in the glass labeled Soda 1 and the other egg in the glass labeled Juice 1. Wash and dry your hands.

5. Gently submerge the remaining eggs, without toothpaste on them, in the remaining glasses: one in the glass labeled Soda 2 and the other in the glass of juice labeled Juice 2. Wash and dry your hands. Leave the eggs in the glasses for 12 hours.

6. After 12 hours, remove the eggs from the glasses of soda one at a time. Rinse them in cool water and pat them dry with the towel. Place each egg by the sticky note of the glass it was in. Are the eggs the same or different colors? Write down your observations in your science notebook.

7. Remove the eggs from the glasses of juice one at a time. Rinse them under the faucet and pat them dry. Place each egg by the sticky note of the glass it was in. Feel the eggs gently. Does one feel stronger or weaker than the other? Write down your observations in your science notebook.

MYSTERY SOLVED! The eggshells in this experiment represent the enamel (outer coating) on your teeth. Toothpaste cleans your teeth and prevents stains: it removes food and drink particles that are stuck on your teeth. Teeth can be stained easily by dark-colored liquids like cola, coffee, or tea. The egg without toothpaste will be brown and discolored. The egg covered in toothpaste was protected from turning brown.

Toothpaste also protects your pearly whites from decay (breaking down). The egg without toothpaste left in the lemon juice was worn down and soft to the touch, while the egg that was protected with toothpaste is stronger. The lemon juice is acidic, and those acids broke down the shell just as acidic drinks can wear away your tooth enamel. When a tooth is worn down, a cavity can form more easily. But the fluoride in toothpaste mixes with your saliva to create a protective coating around your tooth enamel. It helps keep your teeth strong and cavity-free.

TAKE 2! Repeat the experiment with other liquids, like chocolate milk, sports drinks, or juices like apple, tomato, or cranberry. Which liquids do you think will cause staining? Which will cause decay?

Stinky Science

Pee-yew! Shoes can get pretty stinky. What causes the smell, and how can you get rid of it? Let's try two methods for making your shoes a little less smelly.

DIFFICULTY: 💪💪💪 **MESS-O-METER:** ✹ ✹ ✹ **TIME: 15 MINUTES HANDS-ON; 48 HOURS TOTAL**

YOU WILL NEED

A pair of stinky shoes

Large resealable plastic bag

Freezer

Science notebook and pencil

1. Take a whiff of the shoes and record your observations in your science notebook.

2. Slip one shoe into the plastic bag, seal it, and place it in the freezer. Leave it in the freezer for 48 hours.

3. Set the other shoe in a dry place outdoors where sunlight can shine directly on it. (Bring the shoe inside at night so it doesn't get damp from morning dew. Set it out in the sunlight again the second day.)

4. Make a prediction in your science notebook—will either of these methods get rid of the smell? Which one will work better and why?

5. After 48 hours, remove the shoe from the freezer. Fetch the other shoe from outside. Smell each one. Do they smell better or worse? Wait an hour, then smell both shoes again. Did one method work better than the other? Record your observations. Were your predictions correct?

MYSTERY SOLVED! A pair of feet has about 250,000 sweat glands. That's a lot of sweat seeping into your shoes! Bacteria thrive in warm, moist places, which is just the environment your sweaty shoes provide. So it's the bacteria from your feet, socks, and shoes that cause your shoes to stink, not the sweat itself.

When you place a shoe in the freezer, bacteria become inactive—they temporarily freeze up. Once the shoe is removed from the freezer and thaws out, the bacteria become active again. That means that although the smell might be gone at first, unfortunately, it will return.

But the UV rays in sunlight break down and kill bacteria, especially on a hot, dry day. Since sunlight can't reach deep into your shoe, this method is most effective at deodorizing the outside of your shoe.

> NOSE-BLINDNESS HAPPENS WHEN YOUR BRAIN RECOGNIZES A COMMON SMELL AS NONTHREATENING AND TURNS OFF THE RECEPTORS FOR THAT ODOR.

TAKE 2! Here's an odor-reducing trick to try. Fill a sock with baking soda and secure the top with a rubber band. Slip the baking soda-filled sock into your shoe so it completely fills the spaces your foot touches. Test this method for 24 hours, then observe the results. Baking soda doesn't kill the bacteria, but it does absorb smells. Baking soda is a base, which helps neutralize the pH of many smells, which are often acidic.

Wish Wash

Think of all the things you touch during the day. Each of those surfaces has germs on it. Gross, right? In this experiment, you'll cover your hands with washable paint, which will represent how germ-covered your hands can be after a long day. Make a prediction in your science notebook: How many seconds will it take to get rid of every last germ from your hands?

YOU WILL NEED

Washable paint

Liquid hand soap

A timer or stopwatch that can measure seconds

Hand towel

Science notebook and pencil

→ Ask a friend to set the timer for you throughout this experiment.

1. While standing over a sink, squirt a quarter-size amount of washable paint into your cupped hand. Rub your hands together until the paint completely covers them. Make sure to get the tops, bottoms, sides, and in between each finger!

2. Let the paint dry for 5 minutes. Don't touch anything!

3. Once the paint is dry, rinse your hands quickly under the water (while scrubbing your hands together) for 3 seconds. Holding your hands over the sink, observe how much paint is still covering them.

4. Add a squirt of soap to your hands then scrub them together for 10 seconds (about the length of the "Happy Birthday" song). Do you see any paint remaining? Which parts of your hands are the toughest to clean?

5. Scrub with soap for 10 more seconds, or until the paint is completely gone. How long did it take? Rinse your hands thoroughly, then dry them with a clean towel. Write down your observations.

YOU CAN USE A BAR OF SOAP TO SOLVE A SQUEAKY DOOR. RUB ANY NON-GLYCERIN SOAP ON THE HINGE, PROBLEM SOLVED!

MYSTERY SOLVED! Soap is a mixture of oils, fats, and water (plus a little bit of salt). Every day, oils and fats build up on your hands. It's totally normal—just grease from everyday activities. But germs stick to these oils and fats. If you simply rinse your hands with water, the oils and fats (and germs) still stick to your hands. That's because oils and water don't mix.

As you learned in the **Rainbow Milk experiment on page 24**, soap likes oil and water. When you lather up your hands with soap, it lifts the grease (and the germs that are stuck to it) from your hands. Then the water rinses it away. By scrubbing for at least 20 seconds, you work up a lather and the friction loosens dirt, oils, and germs from your skin.

TAKE 2! Try this experiment again, but instead of using soap and water, rub or spray hand sanitizer onto your hands for 20 seconds. How effective is it at removing the paint?

GH WELLNESS LAB +

OUR EXPERT SAYS

"You should lather up frequently, especially:

- When using the bathroom.
- Before you prepare food, and after you've finished eating.
- After you've been outdoors or played with pets.
- After touching something that's widely used, like a doorknob.

Germs can be more easily spread to and from wet hands, so be sure to dry off, too."

—Birnur Aral

Director, Health, Beauty & Environmental Sciences Lab

FAB FACTS ABOUT YUCKY STUFF

Toe Cheese

Different kinds of bacteria are used to help transform milk into cheese. For example, some bacteria are used to grow mold to create blue cheese, and others form curds to make cottage cheese. Other cheeses are washed in a warm and salty solution called brine, which attracts bacteria. As the bacteria eat away at the cheese, they release an odor—sometimes a very strong one. There's a type of cheese called Limburger that people say smells like stinky feet!

Dirty Dollars

Paper money is covered with bacteria. That's not surprising, since bills travel from person to person over a lifespan of 10 or more years. Scientists have found thousands of different types of microbes, from skin cells to fecal matter (ew!). Your skin provides protection, but it's a good idea to wash your hands after handling cash.

That Bites!

Your skin has 2 million to 4 million sweat glands that release a salty liquid called sweat. Its main function is to cool down your body. Sweat is odorless, but bacteria on your skin mix with it, creating a powerful smelly scent. This is what attracts hungry mosquitos.

Sandy Bottoms

A colorful tropical reef dweller called a parrotfish uses its many strong teeth to grind up hard bits of algae-covered coral. It digests the algae, and the coral travels through the fish's digestive system. A single parrotfish can excrete 1,000 pounds (450 kg) of sand in a year. That means the sand you wiggle your toes in might actually be parrotfish poop!

Favorable Flavor

Whether yellow or brown, white or red, onions are versatile veggies that add vitamins, minerals, antioxidants, and fiber to your plate. They can help protect your heart, immune system, and more. They contain sulfur-based compounds that may affect your breath and body odor because they take a while to metabolize. Once they do, the smell will go away.

Shiny and Slimy

Slugs are masterful producers of mucus. Scientists classify this slippery substance, which is both a liquid and a solid, as a liquid crystal (a state of matter between liquid and solid). Mucus helps slugs ooze along as they travel. It also acts like a glue to hold them in place, making it hard for a predator to grab hold. The mucus that comes out of your nose is a liquid crystal, too. It is part of a healthy body, keeping things moist and trapping dust, allergens, bacteria, and viruses. More mucus when you have a cold? That's your body working to protect you.

Sniff Test

Unlike fragrances that cover up bad smells with more pleasant scents, some natural and manufactured items work to eliminate odors. And—whether they come in the form of a spray, a plug-in, or an object that hooks onto the air vent in a car—some odor eliminators trap and neutralize lingering smells by breaking down the compounds that caused the smell in the first place. That's amazing science!

Air Pockets

When raindrops land, most mix into an already wet surface. But not always. As rain falls, air pressure from below pushes upward, flattening the bottoms of the drops. If a thin layer of air gets trapped between the flattened drop bottom and the wet surface, the drop will bead up or bounce, like on an umbrella or rain jacket.

Chapter 7

EXPLORE OUTDOORS

When you go outside, there's dirt beneath your feet (or underneath a sidewalk or roadway). That's Earth's uppermost layer. When you look around, you may spot some pretty flowers or a promising vegetable garden. And if you look up, there's a warm sun, clouds, or precipitation like rain or snow. The experiments in this chapter reveal what's going on in nature that you can't see with the naked eye. Take a deep breath of fresh air and step out into the biggest science laboratory of all.

EXPERIMENTS

Big Muddy

Soil contains water, tiny living organisms, minerals, gases such as oxygen and carbon dioxide, and organic matter (plant and animal material that is in the process of being broken down). It forms the top layer of Earth's surface. Try this experiment to get the dirt on dirt.

DIFFICULTY: 💪💪💪   MESS-O-METER: ✳ ✳ ✳   TIME: 20 MINUTES HANDS-ON; 80 MINUTES TOTAL

YOU WILL NEED

Spoon

1 cup loose soil

Glass jar with a lid, at least 16 ounces (475 ml)

Water

Science notebook and pencil

Timer or stopwatch

1. In a backyard or a park, use a spoon to scoop soil into the jar until it's about halfway full. It's okay if it has a mix of small rocks or leaves.

2. What does the soil in your glass jar look like? Can you see the different components of the soil? Is there more of one component than others? What colors do you see? Record your observations and draw what you see in your science notebook.

3. Pour enough water into the jar to fill it up, leaving a 1-inch (2.5-cm) space at the top. Screw on the lid. Place the jar on a counter. Observe the contents of the jar and record what you see in your science notebook.

4. What does the soil-and-water mixture look like? What color is it? Draw a picture in your science notebook.

5. Carefully shake the jar, then set it back on the counter. Watch what happens right after you set the jar down. Record your observations. Set the timer for 15 minutes.

6. When the 15 minutes are up, check the jar again. Do the contents look different? Record your observations. Continue to set the timer for 15 minutes, check on the jar, and write down your observations twice more. After an hour, what do you see inside the jar? Did anything happen to the components of the soil? What color is the water?

ADOBE, A BRICK MADE FROM MUD, IS USED TO BUILD HOMES AROUND THE WORLD.

ADOBE IS OFTEN USED IN HOT CLIMATES, WHERE IT HELPS KEEP HOMES COOL.

MYSTERY SOLVED! Soil has many different parts, some of which are arranged in layers and some of which are all mixed up. In this experiment, you identified the components of topsoil— the uppermost layer—by creating what scientists call a soil profile. It shows how much of each ingredient the soil contains. The minerals in soil are divided into three groups, based on size: sand is made up of the largest particles, silt is in the middle, and clay has the smallest particles. Depending on where you live, your soil might have more of one ingredient than another.

After you added water to the jar, layers began to form. Each layer is called a horizon. The heavier, larger pieces fall to the bottom, while the smaller ones float to the top. In your jar, rocks or gravel form the bottom layer. The next layer up is the sand, followed by silt, then clay. On top, you may see some things floating in the water—this is the organic matter. You likely noticed that the water is not clear anymore. It looks muddy because minerals from the soil have dissolved in it.

TAKE 2! Let the jar sit for 24 hours without shaking or moving it. Then observe the layers to see if there are any changes. Are there more layers or fewer layers, or are the layers more distinct? Has the water become more or less cloudy? Write down your observations in your science notebook.

Go, Go, Re-Grow!

Do you need seeds and a garden, or even a pot of soil, to grow vegetables? In this experiment you're going to try growing vegetables without seeds or soil. Do you think it's possible? Make a prediction in your science notebook and give it a try.

DIFFICULTY: 💪💪💪   MESS-O-METER: ✺ ✺ ✺   TIME: 15 MINUTES HANDS-ON; 10 DAYS TOTAL

YOU WILL NEED

Science notebook and pencil

Knife (ask an adult to use the knife)

1 stalk celery

1 scallion

1 head romaine lettuce

Ruler

2 small bowls or plastic containers

Water at room temperature

Narrow glass or jar

→ A whole head is called a stalk—one piece is a rib.

SET ASIDE THE LOOSE CELERY RIBS, SCALLION GREENS, AND LETTUCE LEAVES FROM STEP 1— YOU CAN EAT THEM FOR A SNACK OR MAKE A TASTY SALAD.

1. Make a chart like this one in your science notebook. During the experiment, you'll be recording what the plants look like and how tall they have grown.

	CELERY		SCALLION		LETTUCE	
	APPEARANCE	HEIGHT	APPEARANCE	HEIGHT	APPEARANCE	HEIGHT
DAY 1						
DAY 4						
DAY 7						
DAY 10						

2. This experiment uses the root ends of vegetables. Ask an adult to cut through the entire celery stalk, including the ribs, 2 inches (5 cm) from the bottom. Then have them cut the scallion 2 inches (5 cm) from the bottom (the end with the roots) and the lettuce head two 2 inches (5 cm) from the bottom.

3. Now it's time to "plant" your veggies. Place the lettuce and celery bases in separate shallow bowls, cut side up. The bowls should be just big enough for the vegetables, so they stay upright. Add enough water to the bowls to cover half of each vegetable, about 1 inch (2.5 cm) or so. Place the scallion root end down in a skinny glass or jar and add water until it comes about 1 inch (2.5 cm) up the side of the glass.

4. Place the vegetable containers near a sunny window. Check on your plants every 3 days and record your observations in your science notebook. Are there signs that the vegetables are growing? What do those signs look like? Measure the vegetables with a ruler and record any changes in height in your science notebook. Is one growing faster than the others? When you check your vegetables, make sure there's always at least 1 inch (2.5 cm) of water in the containers and add water if needed. Change the water every 2 or 3 days to make sure it stays fresh.

5. At the end of 10 days, compare your final results. Which veggie grew the fastest? The tallest? The slowest? Complete the chart in your science notebook.

NOTE IT! If some of your veggies didn't grow, that's okay. Variables such as air temperature, amount of sunlight, and even how fresh the vegetables were when you started can make a difference. Try again and see if you get different results.

MYSTERY SOLVED! Within 3 to 4 days, your vegetable scraps should start to grow. After 7 days, the lettuce should have new leaves, the scallion should have grown taller, and the celery should have begun to sprout leaves and grown taller. You may have noticed some roots growing out from the bottoms of the celery and scallion. The scallion most likely grew the fastest and tallest.

Plants make their own food from a combination of water, sunlight, and gases in the air. This is a chemical process called photosynthesis. During this process, plants absorb water, usually, but not always, from soil; light from the sun; and a gas called carbon dioxide from the air. They turn those ingredients into a type of sugar called glucose, which the plant then breaks down into energy that it uses to grow. The plant releases oxygen into the air when it breaks down glucose. When you put those vegetable parts in water and placed them in a sunny spot, they had everything they needed to grow.

TAKE 2! Continue the experiment for an additional week, changing the water every 2 or 3 days. Do the vegetables continue to grow? Record your observations.

Go with the Flow

When freshly cut flowers are put into a vase filled with water, does the water stay in the vase, does it evaporate completely, or does something else happen? Discover exactly what's going on and how water helps flowers stay fresh.

DIFFICULTY: 💪💪💪   MESS-O-METER: ✸ ✸ ✸   TIME: 15 MINUTES HANDS-ON; 24 HOURS TOTAL

YOU WILL NEED

2 narrow same-size glasses or jars

Water

Blue and red food coloring

Spoon

3 white carnations

Sharp knife or scissors (ask an adult to use the knife or scissors)

Ruler

Science notebook and pencil

Timer or stopwatch

→ Thicker flower stems are easier to cut, but ask an adult to help regardless.

1. Fill each glass halfway with warm water and set the glasses side by side on a counter or table. Add 20 drops of blue food coloring to one glass and stir with the spoon. Add 20 drops of red food coloring to the other glass and stir.

2. Ask an adult to trim the bottoms of the stems of all three carnations so that they will stand up about 2 inches (5 cm) above the rim of the glasses or jars.

3. On one of the flowers, ask the adult to cut or slice the stem down the middle lengthwise, starting at the bottom. The cut needs to stop about 1 inch (2.5 cm) below the flower. Don't split the stems of the other two flowers.

4. Place one uncut flower stem in each glass. For the flower with the split stem, place half of the stem in each glass.

5. Over time, what will happen to the color of each carnation? Make a prediction in your science notebook. If you think they will change colors, what colors do you think they will become? Now comes the hard part: waiting! Set the timer for 30 minutes.

6. Check on your flowers every 30 minutes over the next 3 hours. What is happening to the carnations? Write down your observations in your science notebook each time you check.

7. Leave the carnations overnight. What happened? Did it match your prediction? Jot the results in your science notebook.

MYSTERY SOLVED! All plants have roots that absorb (take in) water from the soil. The water moves upward—the exact *opposite* of the force of gravity—from the roots, through the stem, to the leaves and, sometimes, to flowers. This process is called capillary action. Freshly cut flowers don't have roots, but they do have stems. When you placed the stems in the water, capillary action brought the water up the stems and into the petals of the flowers. The food coloring made this process visible.

The carnations likely began to change colors in 3 hours or less. (Flowers with shorter stems will absorb the water more quickly because it has a shorter distance to travel.) Did you predict that the carnation with the split stem—half in each color—would would turn purple because that's the usual result when you mix blue and red? You might have been surprised that the flower didn't actually turn purple. Instead, one half turned blue and the other half turned red. That's because each color of food coloring followed its own path up the stem and into the flower.

TAKE 2! Can you make a rainbow of flowers? Try mixing different colors in glasses of water—red and yellow to make orange, yellow and blue to make green, red and blue to make purple. Can you make pink by using fewer drops of red food coloring? Will yellow show up on flower petals? Then add a white flower to each glass. Observe them over 24 hours. Where does the color first appear? Now observe them after 5 days. Are the colors paler or brighter?

Make It Rain

When dark clouds gather in the sky, one thing's for sure: it's going to rain sometime soon. But when? And why? Try this experiment to learn what's going on inside a rain cloud *before* it rains.

DIFFICULTY:  MESS-O-METER: TIME: 15 MINUTES

YOU WILL NEED

1 16-ounce (473-ml) clear glass or plastic jar

Measuring cup

Water

Shaving cream

Liquid food coloring (1 or several colors)

Small cup (1 for each color you use)

Spoon

Eyedropper

Science notebook and pencil

1. Pour 1½ cups (354 ml) of water into the jar. Add shaving cream to the jar, filling it just to the top. This is your cloud.

2. Decide whether you want to use one color for your rain or a few different colors. For each color you decide to use, fill a small cup with water.

3. Add 3 drops of food coloring to one of the cups. Stir to combine. If you are using more than one color, repeat this step with the other colors. (See image A.)

4. Place the eyedropper in a cup of colored water and squeeze the dropper top to collect some of the liquid. (See image B.) Squeeze a drop of the liquid onto the shaving cream. Observe what happens. Add a few more drops. Does anything happen?

5. If you're using more than one color, switch to the next color and start adding drops of it to your shaving cream cloud. Does anything happen? Keep adding drops of colored water to your shaving cream cloud, a few at a time. (See image C.) How many drops does it take before your cloud starts to "rain" into the water below? Record your results in your science notebook.

MYSTERY SOLVED! Clouds are made up mostly of water droplets, but why do they only sometimes release the droplets as rain? When too many droplets gather in a cloud, they condense (join) and become heavy. When they become too heavy, the force of gravity pulls the droplets toward Earth and they fall from the cloud as rain (or snow or hail).

In this experiment, the shaving cream acted like a cloud. It held droplets of colored water until it got too full. When enough water droplets came together in your shaving cream cloud, they were too heavy for the cloud to hold and were pulled down into the water—just like rain falling in the sky.

TAKE 2! Use a bigger jar or container and make your shaving cream cloud bigger and taller. Add the same number of drops of colored water to the cloud. Observe what happens. Will you need more or fewer drops to get the rain to fall? Record your observations in your science notebook.

RAINDROPS ARE DOME-SHAPED— ROUND ON THE TOP AND FLAT ON THE BOTTOM.

LIKE ME!

Time Teller

To find out the time, you can easily look at a clock, a watch, or a smartphone. But how did people know the time of day before these inventions? All they needed was the sun and a few natural materials to estimate the time. In this experiment, you'll make your own time-telling device—a sundial.

DIFFICULTY: 🦾🦾🦾   MESS-O-METER: ✷ ✷ ✷   TIME: 30 MINUTES HANDS-ON; 24 HOURS TOTAL

YOU WILL NEED

Bright-color permanent marker (1 or several colors)

12 pale-colored rocks (small to medium)

Sunny, outdoor space

Ruler or tape measure

Straight stick or twig with small branches removed, about 12 inches (30 cm) long

Modeling clay (if you're using a solid surface instead of the ground)

Science notebook and pencil

Watch, clock, or smartphone

→ This experiment works best if you set up your sundial in a place where it will be not be disturbed for at least 24 hours.

1. Using the permanent marker(s), number the rocks from 1 through 12.

2. Find a sunny outdoor place with enough room to construct your sundial. You'll need an area about 2 feet by 2 feet (61 cm by 61 cm). Measure the space with your ruler or tape measure.

3. If you are building the sundial on grass or dirt, insert your stick into the ground in the middle of the space. If you are working on a solid surface (like pavement or a balcony), place a lump of clay about the size of your fist on the hard surface. Insert your stick into the clay so that it stands upright. Use more clay if needed to hold the stick upright.

4. The stick should be casting a shadow on the ground. Can you see it? Which direction is the sunlight coming from? Is the sun low or high in the sky right now? Record your observations in your science notebook.

5. Now check the time on a watch. On the hour (for example, at exactly 9 a.m.), pick up the numbered rock that matches the hour and place it on the ground in the path of the stick's shadow. Move the rock so that it is 8 to 10 inches (20 to 25 cm) from the center stick and still in the path of the shadow, using your ruler or tape measure to measure.

6. Place the other rocks even distances apart, forming a circle around the stick. They should follow numerical order, just as you would see on the face of a clock. So place the 10 to the right of the 9, then the 11, and so on. Now make a prediction in your science notebook: Which way do you think the shadow will move? Why do you think the shadow will move that way?

7. Check your sundial in exactly 1 hour. If you started at 9 a.m., then at 10 a.m. is the shadow touching the rock that says 10? If not, move the 10 rock slightly so that it falls in the path of the shadow. (If you started at a different time, the shadow should have moved to the next rock to the right.) Continue to do this

for each hour of sunlight, adjusting the position of the rocks as necessary. Then start early the next morning and adjust any remaining numbers. Now you've adjusted the rocks over 12 hours of daylight.

8. Using your ruler, measure the distances between the rocks—are they the same distance from one another? Is your circle perfectly round or is it a somewhat imperfect shape? Record your observations in your science notebook.

9. Keep checking on your clock each hour. How accurate is your sundial in telling the time? How is a sundial different from a typical watch?

MYSTERY SOLVED! During the course of a day, the sun rises in the east in the early morning, is overhead around noon (12 p.m.), and then sets in the west around dinnertime. As Earth rotates on its axis, the sun appears to move across the sky. The shadow cast by the stick moves as the position of the sun moves, and shows the time of day. The sundial indicates solar time, which is your local time based on the position of the sun relative to Earth.

In a sundial, the center stick is called the gnomon (*NO-men*). The gnomon's shadow is like the hour hand on a watch. A sundial doesn't have separate hour and minute hands, but you can guess about what time it is based on the shadow that is cast by the gnomon. For example, if the shadow is halfway between 9 and 10, then it's around 9:30. The season and where you live on Earth will determine what your sundial looks like. The distance between each rock might not be exactly equal, and your sundial might not be a perfect circle.

TAKE 2! Leave your sundial where it is and consult it over the next few days. Compare the sundial's reading in the morning with a clock or watch, and try again in the late afternoon. When was it able to tell the exact time? Were there any times in the day when it was a little bit off?

Wave Works

What makes waves move and why? First, make a prediction in your science notebook: How do you think waves work? What causes them to move and crash onto beaches around the world every day? Or to slosh against the sides of your bathtub? Then take a look at what happens in this experiment.

DIFFICULTY: 💪💪💪 MESS-O-METER: ✳ ✳ ✳ TIME: 10 MINUTES

YOU WILL NEED

1 empty 16.9-ounce (500-ml) plastic water or soda bottle (cleaned, label removed)

Water

3 drops blue food coloring

1 14-ounce (414-ml) bottle of baby oil

Funnel

Science notebook and pencil

1. Fill the bottle with ¾ cup (177 ml) of water. Add the food coloring. Screw on the cap, then shake the bottle to combine the food coloring and water.

2. Remove the cap and, using the funnel, add the baby oil to the bottle. Fill the bottle to about ½ inch (13 mm) from the top. Screw the cap on firmly.

3. Place one hand on either end of the bottle and turn it sideways. Let the oil and water settle (stop moving), then slowly tilt the ends up and down in a gentle seesaw motion. Does the water move the same way the bottle moves? Record your observations in your science notebook.

4. Tilt the bottle back and forth more quickly, then stop suddenly and hold the bottle still. Keep an eye on the water. Did it stop moving when you stopped tilting the bottle, or did it keep moving? Record your observations.

MYSTERY SOLVED!

When you tilted the bottle slightly from side to side, the water was pulled by gravity toward whichever side was tilted downward. This created wave action. Tidal waves—waves that form in shallow waters (like shorelines) of the ocean—are caused by gravity, too. Oceans swell (move) because of the gravitational force of the moon as it revolves around Earth. The sun's gravitational force interacting with Earth also causes waves in the ocean. As Earth rotates on its axis, different sides turn toward the moon, and the tides go in and out.

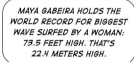

MAYA GABEIRA HOLDS THE WORLD RECORD FOR BIGGEST WAVE SURFED BY A WOMAN: 73.5 FEET HIGH. THAT'S 22.4 METERS HIGH.

THAT'S TALLER THAN FOUR GIRAFFES STANDING ON TOP OF ONE ANOTHER.

FAB FACTS ABOUT NATURE

Outdoor Gear

More than a thousand years before there were smartphones, there were astrolabes. These complex devices were used to tell the time, navigate using the sun and the stars, do mathematical calculations, and even measure the position of Earth on its axis. That's smart!

Bee Good

Flowers may not look busy, but they work with bees to help put food on your dinner table. When bees drink nectar from a flower, pollen sticks to their legs and bodies. As they move from flower to flower, they collect pollen from one and deposit it on another. This process, called cross-pollination, is necessary for some plants to develop seeds that grow into new plants. Honeybees fertilize more than two-thirds of the crops that people eat, including strawberries, apples, watermelons, broccoli, string beans, and almonds.

Standing Tall

Redwoods are the tallest trees in the world. They can grow to more than 300 feet (92 m) tall. The tallest of all Redwoods is called Hyperion—it rises more than 380 feet (116 m) into the sky in northern California. These trees can live for a couple thousand years—that's a long time to keep growing!

Luminous Lights

When the night sky lights up around the North or South Pole with a curtain of colors—blue, red, yellow, orange, green—it's called an aurora. An aurora occurs when solar wind, which is a stream of charged particles (ions) from the sun, hits Earth's magnetic field. Some of the ions collide with oxygen and nitrogen atoms in the atmosphere. The collisions cause energy to be released in the form of colored light.

Super Power

How is it possible that the brown recluse spider's silk is 1,000 times thinner than a human hair yet five times stronger than steel? Each strand of its silk is reinforced with micro-loops (about 20 loops for every millimeter/0.04 inch). It's tough and elastic—it can stretch easily, rather than break.

Wiggle Room

There are more than 7,000 different species (types) of earthworms, and they improve soil where they live. They eat debris and expel whatever they can't digest back into the soil, providing rich nutrients for plants. They loosen and aerate soil and improve drainage. These wiggling wonders even create channels for roots to grow.

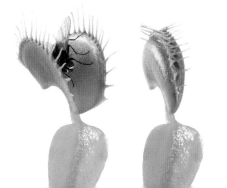

Open Wide

The leaves of a Venus flytrap plant grow in hinged pairs that sit open, waiting for a tasty treat to come by. The edges have short teethlike hairs that are sensitive to motion. When they sense an insect or a spider moving around, the leaves snap closed, trapping it inside. Digestive juices break down the prey. It can take a week or longer for the plant to complete its meal.

Glossary

acid A substance that has a pH of less than 7 and, in foods like lemons and vinegar, tastes sour.

air pressure The weight of air molecules as they press down on Earth.

atom The basic building block of matter. All matter (including you!) is made up of atoms.

bacteria Single-celled microscopic living things. Bacteria grow all around you, including on many surfaces in your home. Some can make a person sick, but others are good for you.

base A substance that has a pH level higher than 7 and, in foods like kale and green tea, tastes bitter.

circuit A closed loop that electricity can travel through.

conductor A material that can have electricity, heat, or sound flow through it.

density A way to measure how tightly packed molecules are.

electricity A form of energy resulting from the flow of charged particles.

electron A tiny particle inside an atom that has a negative charge.

energy The ability of a person or a machine to do work; the power to make things move or change.

evaporation The process of a substance changing from a liquid into a vapor (a substance that floats in the air).

fluid A substance that easily changes its shape and that flows.

force A push or a pull that makes something move, stop, or change direction.

frequency How quickly or slowly waves of energy (like sound waves or light waves) move.

friction Resistance created when one surface moves over another surface; a force that sometimes slows things down.

fulcrum The point where a lever turns or balances.

gas A state of matter without a fixed shape that can expand (get bigger) or contract (get smaller), such as air.

gravity A force that pulls masses toward one another and keeps them from floating apart. On Earth, gravity pulls matter downward.

kinetic energy Energy an object has because of its motion. A bouncing ball has kinetic energy.

liquid A state of matter that does not have a clearly defined shape and can flow, such as water.

mass How much matter something contains.

matter Anything that takes up space, including solids, liquids, and gases.

mixture A combination of two or more substances that can be separated into their original parts. A tossed salad and mud (water and dirt) are examples of mixtures.

molecule A combination of two or more atoms.

motion When an object changes position or location.

neutron A particle inside an atom that has a neutral charge (is neither positive nor negative).

Newtonian fluid A liquid whose viscosity (ability to flow) never changes; the viscosity of a non-Newtonian fluid can change.

organism Any living thing, such as a tree, a rabbit, or mold.

pH level A measure of how acidic or basic a liquid is.

photosynthesis The process of plants getting energy by making their food from light, water, and carbon dioxide.

pitch How high or low a sound is.

polar molecule A molecule with a positive charge at one end and a negative charge at the other end.

potential energy The stored energy an object has when it is not moving. A pencil on a desk has potential energy. (When it's falling to the floor, it has kinetic energy.)

proton A particle inside an atom that has a positive charge.

reaction When two or more things—such as chemicals, atoms, objects, or forces—act on each other and are changed in some way.

resistance A force that pushes against another force.

simple machine A device that has few or no moving parts and is used to change the movement of an object or make a force stronger: axle, wheel, inclined plane, lever, pulley, wedge, or screw. A compound machine—such as a pair of scissors or a crane—combines two or more simple machines.

solid A state of matter that's rigid, feels hard, and has a clearly defined shape.

soluble A substance that can be dissolved in a liquid, especially water; insoluble substances cannot be dissolved in a liquid.

static electricity An electric charge produced by friction.

vegan A product that doesn't contain any ingredients that come from an animal; a person who doesn't eat animal products.

volume The amount of space an object or a substance takes up, including its height, width, and length.

vortex A swirling mass, such as a tornado or whirlpool.

wavelength The distance between waves of energy (such as sound waves or light waves).

S.T.E.A.M. Index

Experiment	Pages	Science	Technology	Engineering	Art	Math
Act Fast!	110-111	x				x
All Puffed Up	30-31	x	x			x
Attract and Repel	102-103	x		x	x	
Big Muddy	138-139	x		x		
Battery Blast	62-65		x	x	x	
Blast Off	82-83	x		x		x
Boing Boing	106-107	x				x
Bubble Buddies	52-53	x		x		
Don't Forget to Brush	128-129	x	x			
Fight the Fog	46-47	x	x	x		
Floating Fish	56-57	x	x	x		
Free Falling	84-85		x	x		
From Smell to Smile	32-33	x				
Giant Bubble Rainbows	50-51	x	x		x	
Go for It!	108-109	x		x		x
Go with the Flow	142-143	x			x	
Go, Go, Re-Grow!	140-141	x	x			
Good Vibrations	88-89	x	x			
Grime Fighters	122-123	x	x			
Let's Bounce	104-105	x	x	x		
Light Energy	66-67	x	x	x	x	
Make It Rain	144-145	x		x		

Experiment	Page	Science	Technology	Engineering	Art	Math
Odd Couples	34-35	x				
Oo-Oo-Oobleck	120-121	x	x		x	
Paper Puzzler	96-99			x		x
Positivity Project	72-73	x	x			
Presto Change-O	28-29	x	x			
Puff Painting	86-87	x		x	x	
Rainbow Milk	24-25	x	x		x	
Shake-and-Make Butter	26-27	x	x			
Shape-Shifter	100-101			x		x
Sink or Float?	48-49		x	x		
Slime Time	118-119	x	x		x	
Solar S'mores	68-71	x	x	x		
Spin Is In	44-45		x	x		
Stinky Science	130-131	x		x		
Strike a Pose	94-95	x				x
Taste It, Test It	36-37	x				
Thicker Picker-Uppers	54-55	x	x	x		
Time Teller	146-147	x	x			
Wave Works	148-149	x				
What Mold Told Us	124-127	x				
Wheel Fun	80-81		x	x		
Wish Wash	132-133	x	x			

Index

PHOTO CREDITS

Top - UP, Center - CTR, Bottom - LO, Left - LE, Right - RT, Background - BG

Cover: Studio D, Philip Friedman BG/Flap UP/Flap CTR/UP LE/UP RT/LO LE/LO RT, ©LisaValder/Getty Flap LO, ©Leanne Irwin/Shutterstock UP CTR, ©Jim Thompson/Zuma Press/agefotostock CTR LE, ©Roman Samborskyi/Shutterstock CTR, ©Jose Luis Pelaez Inc/Getty CTR RT

Our Experts and Lab Assistants: Studio D, Chris Eckert (6, 8 UP, 9 UP), Mike Garten (8 LO, 9 LO, 10 UP, 10 LO, 11 LO, NXM Photo (11 UP); ©m-imagephotography/Getty (24 LO), ©LightFieldStudios/Getty (31), ©Tom Chance/Getty (34 RT), ©JBryson/Getty (44 LE), ©Antonio_Diaz/Getty (44 RT), ©drbimages/Getty (50), ©ajijchan/Getty (52); ©yopinco/Getty (6-11, 24, 31, 34 RT, 44 LE/RT, 50, 52, 56, 66, 70 LE/RT, 80, 82, 84, 88, 94, 96, 101, 102, 104, 106, 108 LE, 110 RT, 118, 138 LE/RT, 144 RT, 148 LE)

Experiments Photoshoot: Studio D, Philip Friedman (1, 2, 25, 29, 31, 37, 45, 47, 49, 55, 57, 64,69, 71, 81, 83, 85, 95, 97, 99, 101, 129, 139, 145, 149)

agefotostock: ©Alan Dawson/agefotostock 21 UP RT, ©James Schwabel 75 LO LE, ©Dave King 89 LO, ©Jim Thompson/Zuma Press 121 RT; **Dreamstime:** ©Holger Geller 53 UP, ©Julia Sudnitskaya 136 BG; **Getty Images:** ©VICTOR DE SCHWANBERG/SCIENCE PHOTO LIBRARY 2 UP RT, ©Digital Vision. 2 CTR, ©Witthaya Prasongsin 2 LO LE, ©Georgijevic 2 LO RT, ©Sunday Times 4 BG, ©Orapan Yenchum/EyeEm 7 UP RT, ©Digital Art 12 UP RT, ©Don White 13 BG, ©Viorika 14 LO LE, ©Getty Images/Cultura RF 15 UP RT, ©RBOZUK 15 LO LE, ©Tahreer Photography 16 UP LE, ©RF Pictures 17 BG, ©ATU Images 18 UP RT, ©Miguel Sotomayor 18 LO LE/LO RT, ©emholk 19 UP LE, ©Creative Crop 19 UP RT, ©lisagagne 19 LO RT, ©Education Images 20 UP LE, ©hudiemm 20 UP RT, ©Theerasak Tammachuen/EyeEm 20 LO RT, ©501452 21 CTR LE, ©YvanDube 21 LO, ©LEONELLO CALVETTI/SCIENCE PHOTO LIBRARY 22 BG, ©inkoly 29 LO CTR, ©JoKMedia 33 UP LE, ©FotografiaBasica 33 UP CTR/CTR RT, ©R.Tsubin 33 UP RT, ©Salih Enes Ozbayoglu 33 CTR UP CTR, ©srpphoto 33 CTR UP RT, ©Michelle Arnold/EyeEm 33 CTR LE/CTR LO RT, ©Floortje 33 CTR, ©princessdlaf 33 CTR LO LE, ©Photo by Cathy Scola 33 CTR LO CTR, ©Mark Lund 33 LO LE, ©Richard Clark 33 LO CTR, ©Photo by marianna armata 33 LO RT, ©Gandee Vasan 34 LO LE, ©Lauren Burke 35 UP LE, ©TokenPhoto 35 UP RT, ©Rosemary Calvert 35 CTR LE, ©CWLawrence 35 CTR RT, ©PLAINVIEW 35 LO LE, ©Maren Caruso 35 LO RT, ©Lorant Csakany/EyeEm 38 UP RT, ©Foodcollection RF 38 CTR RT, ©Henrik Weis 38 LO LE, ©Sasi Ponchaisang/EyeEm 38 LO RT, ©"Lscher, Sabine" 39 UP LE, ©Juan Algar Carrascosa/EyeEm 39 CTR, ©eyetoeyePIX 39 CTR RT, ©Arx0nt 39 LO LE, ©ALEAIMAGE 40 CTR LE, ©Andreas Berheide/EyeEm 40 LO CTR/LO RT, ©Magnascan 41 UP RT, ©James Schneider/EyeEm 41 LO RT, ©Carol Yepes 51 BG, ©Jobalou 58 UP RT, ©LOVE_LIFE 58 CTR LE, ©C Squared Studios 58 CTR RT, ©George Doyle 58 LO RT, ©JoeLena 58 LO CTR/LO RT, ©anilyanik 59 UP LE, ©janrysavy 59 LO RT, ©Shannon Fagan 59 LO RT, ©peepo 60 BG/153 CTR UP, ©Jose Luis Pelaez Inc 73 BG, ©Peter Smith/EyeEm 74 LO, ©Camerique 75 UP RT, ©Chris UPher Morris - Corbis 75 LO RT, ©Leontura 76 UP LE/UP CTR RT/UP RT, ©Reggie Casagrande 76 LO RT, ©AFP/Staff 77 UP RT, ©FreeTransform 77 CTR LE 1/LO LE 1, ©FingerMedium 77 CTR LE 2/LO LE 2, ©Thinkstock Images 77 LO RT, ©MirageC 78 BG/153 UP, ©ruizluquepaz 87 RT, ©Laura Hedien 90 UP LE, ©pixhook 90 UP RT, ©Don Farrall 90 LO LE/151 LO LE/LO CTR, ©Rubberball/Mark Anderson 90 LO RT, ©Graiki 91 UP LE, ©Mel Yates 91 LO LE, ©JaCZhou 2015 91 LO RT, ©Andriy Onufriyenko 92 BG/153 CTR LO, ©cyoginan 95 LO RT, ©MediaProduction 98 UP LE, ©CGinspiration 103 LO LE, ©AnthiaCumming 105 LO RT, ©MarcBruxelle 107 UP RT, ©DNY59 111 LO RT, ©MamiEva 112 UP RT, ©Gary Burke 112 CTR LE, ©Rob Lewine 112 LO LE, ©Vudhikul Ocharoen/EyeEm 112 LO RT, ©Fuse 113 UP LE/CTR, ©LisaValder 113 CTR LE, ©Geri Lavrov 113 LO RT, ©Michael Dodge/Stringer 114 UP LE, ©Sorapop Udomsri/EyeEm 115 RT, ©Sunday Times 119 BG, ©John_Brueske 123 LO RT, ©KATERYNA KON/SCIENCE PHOTO LIBRARY 125 UP RT, ©Frank Bean 125 BG, ©Amir Mukhtar 126 LO RT, ©Kwanchai Chai-Udom/EyeEm 131 LO RT, ©PeopleImages 133 LO RT, ©NoDerog 134 CTR, ©Bernard Lynch 134 LO LE, ©Federica Grassi 134 LO RT, ©Suzifoo 135 UP LE, ©Smith Collection/Gado 135 CTR, ©Science Photo Library 135 RT, ©Jeffrey Coolidge 143 LO RT, ©cris180 144 LO LE, ©hidesy 147 LO LE, ©prapassong 148 LO RT, ©jodiecoston 150 UP LE, ©Kerrick 150 UP RT, ©Sumiko Scott 150 LO LE, ©Noppawat Tom Charoensinphon 151 UP LE, ©Schiz-Art 151 UP RT, ©Flavio Coelho 151 CTR; **Shutterstock:** ©Vivida Photo PC 2 UP RT, ©Designua 12 CTR UP RT/CTR LO RT/LO RT, ©OSweetNature 14 UP RT, ©a_v_d 16 LO RT, ©GlobalMediaArt 19 LO LE, ©ChrisVanLennepPhoto 20 LO RT, ©curiosity 27 BG/37 BG/47 BG/55 BG/65 BG/103 BG/105 BG/127 BG/131 BG/133 BG/147 BG, ©Gts 33 CTR UP LE, ©STROBE 42 BG, ©Vangert 56 LO LE, ©MarySan 63 LO LE/65 LO CTR, ©Chester-Alive 67 CTR, ©BlueRingMedia 74 UP LE, ©Suz7 76 UP CTR LE, ©Lucian Coman 77 UP LE, ©Friends Stock 107 LO RT, ©Roman Samborskyi 109 RT, ©Jne Valokuvaus 114 LO LE, ©Alina Tanya 116 BG/153 LO, ©Pedora Alexandra 134 UP LE, ©Leanne Irwin 141 UP RT; **The Noun Project:** ©Leszek Pietrzak 7 UP LE, ©kareemovic2000 7 CTR LE, ©Roberto Chiaveri 7 LO LE; **Endpapers:** ©curiosity/Shutterstock BG

Book produced by **SCOUT** BOOKS&MEDIA
President: Susan Knopf
Editor: Beth Adelman
Researcher: Kimberly Holcombe
Art director and designer: Dirk Kaufman
Photo retoucher: Ruth Vazquez

Special thanks to the testing crew, including Lily Stein, James Stein, Richard Stein, Elizabeth Guidi, and Mark Charles; and gratitude to Jesse Kasehagen, 7th grade science teacher at Santa Barbara Middle School and advocate of project-based learning, for his expertise and guidance.

Library of Congress Cataloging-in-Publication Data Available on request

10 9 8 7 6 5 4 3 2 1

WOW! A LOT OF PEOPLE WORKED ON THIS BOOK!

kids HEARST HOME

Published by Hearst Home Kids
An imprint of Hearst Books
Hearst Magazine Media, Inc.
300 W 57th Street
New York, NY 10019

Good Housekeeping, the Good Housekeeping logo, Hearst Home Kids, the Hearst Home Kids logo, and Hearst Books are registered trademarks of Hearst Communications, Inc.

For information about custom editions, special sales, premium and corporate purchases: hearst.com/magazines/hearst-books

Printed in Canada

ISBN 978-1-950785-89-6